THE
ELECTRIC WAR

EDISON, TESLA, WESTINGHOUSE, *and the* RACE TO LIGHT THE WORLD

To my il
of whom
e Mese

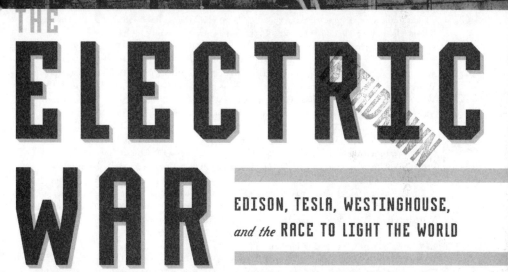

THE ELECTRIC WAR

WAR

EDISON, TESLA, WESTINGHOUSE,
and the RACE TO LIGHT THE WORLD

MIKE WINCHELL

Christy Ottaviano Books
HENRY HOLT AND COMPANY • NEW YORK

Henry Holt and Company, *Publishers since 1866*
Henry Holt® is a registered trademark of Macmillan Publishing Group, LLC.
175 Fifth Avenue, New York, NY 10010 • mackids.com

Photograph pp. ii–iii: 'Nikola Tesla, with his equipment for.' Credit: Wellcome Collection. CC BY. p. 72: Thomas Edison and his original dynamo, courtesy of the Library of Congress. All other images Wikimedia Commons. p. 6: William Kemler; p. 16: electric chair; p. 19: Thomas Edison2-crop; p. 23: young Thomas Edison; p. 41: pióro elektryczne; pp. 42–43: HD.11.031_(10995366585); p. 56: Thomas Edison Glühbirne; p. 70: Edison Machine Works Goerck Street New York 1881; p. 83: NikoTS; p. 86: a new system of alternating current motors and transformers 09; p. 95: by Romain Ramier; p. 96: Teslabulb; p. 99: by Romain Ramier; p. 101: William Arnold Anthony; p. 104 (left): system of electric lighting-Nikola Tesla US patent 454622 fig1; p. 104 (right): rmfpatent; p. 107: Tesla3; p. 108: George Westinghouse; p. 115: L'Illustration 1862 gravure Percement du Mont Cenis 04, Entrée du tunnel; p. 116: Westinghouse air brake control handle and valve; p. 131: Blizzard 1888 01; p. 152: Execution by Electricity electric chair illustration Scientific American Volumes 58–59 June 30 1888; p. 185: elementary two phase alternator; p. 188: map of the 1893 World's Columbian Exposition by Rand Mcnally; p. 189: Westinghouse dynamo 1893 fair machinery building; p. 190: Court of Honor 1893 World Fair; p. 191: Chi Fair Statue of the Republic; p. 192: original Ferris; p. 195: World's Columbian Exposition Administration BuildingS03i2155l01; p. 197: S03 06 01 016 image 2178; p. 199: WorldsFairTeslaPresentation; pp. 200–201: Interior of Electricity Building-official views of the World's Columbian Exposition-30; p. 218: Westinghouse generators at Niagara Falls; p. 224: Topsy elephant death electrocution at Luna Park 1903; p. 226: TeslaWirelessPower1891; p. 227: Wardenclyffe Tower-1904; p. 229: Brochure-Wardenclyffe; p. 230: Nikola tesla in laboratorul sau; p. 232: Kinetoscope

Library of Congress Cataloging-in-Publication Data
Names: Winchell, Mike, author.
Title: The electric war : Edison, Tesla, Westinghouse and the race to light the world / Mike Winchell.
Description: First edition. | New York : Henry Holt and Company, 2019. | "Christy Ottaviano Books." | Audience: Ages 12–14. | Includes bibliographical references and index.
Identifiers: LCCN 2018021059 | ISBN 9781250120168 (hardcover)
Subjects: LCSH: Edison, Thomas A. (Thomas Alva), 1847-1931—Juvenile literature. | Tesla, Nikola, 1856-1943—Juvenile literature. | Westinghouse, George, 1846-1914—Juvenile literature. | Electrification—History—Juvenile literature. | Electric power—History—Juvenile literature. | Electrical engineering—United States—History—Juvenile literature. | Lighting—United States—History—Juvenile literature. | Inventors—United States—Juvenile literature.
Classification: LCC TK140.E3 W478 2019 | DDC 621.3/09—dc23
LC record available at https://lccn.loc.gov/2018021059

Our books may be purchased in bulk for promotional, educational, or business use. Please contact your local bookseller or the Macmillan Corporate and Premium Sales Department at (800) 221-7945 ext. 5442 or by email at MacmillanSpecialMarkets@macmillan.com.

First edition, 2019 / Designed by Carol Ly
Printed in the United States of America
10 9 8 7 6 5 4 3 2 1

For Shelby, A.J., and Savannah:
My everything

CONTENTS

THE
ELECTRIC WAR

EDISON, TESLA, WESTINGHOUSE, *and the* RACE TO LIGHT THE WORLD

·· INTRODUCTION ··

The Gilded Age. The time period of the late nineteenth century when innovation had become big business, the next colossal invention could belong to anyone, and society itself was the battleground. The United States had established itself as an industrial superpower, leading many to say the country was run more by the patent office than by the government.

But with this boom in innovation, man was pitted against man, and a cutthroat race was on to create the newest and most profound advancements in civilization since the wheel, like the light bulb and electric current. Be the first, and fame and fortune were yours. Be the second, and nothing, just anonymity and wishful thinking. Sabotage, conspiracy, scandal, public execution . . . everything was fair play on the Gilded Age battlefield, which matched genius against genius, scholar against scholar. Winner takes all.

With this as a backdrop, the key showdown found Thomas Edison and his firmly established direct current system of electricity pitted head-to-head against Nikola Tesla and George Westinghouse and their innovative and experimental alternating current system. The stakes were as high as they could be, since both sides knew almost every new invention that came along would be powered by whichever system won the battle. And since everything was turning to electric power, whoever won this competition would virtually run the world.

This is the story of three prominent men of the Gilded Age: Thomas Edison, Nikola Tesla, and George Westinghouse. It's about who they were as individuals, what they did to advance society, how they worked to hone and improve their inventions, and ultimately, what they did to try to best their competition and win the battle.

With regard to the treatment of animals represented in this book, the depictions portrayed will understandably be disturbing to many readers. Today we have strict laws pertaining to the humane treatment of animals. During the Gilded Age, however, the American Society for the Prevention of Cruelty to Animals (ASPCA) was still relatively young in its development, having only been established in 1866. The descriptions of animal abuse by Harold P. Brown and others in this book are an unfortunate reminder of two realities of the Gilded Age. First, it signified the dire need to strengthen the laws and regulations to help protect animals from abuse. Second, it showed the lengths these men would go to in the name of competition.

While the narrative chronicles the forces that drove these titans to the height of their craft, there is much more to share than the formative experiences and upbringing of each inventor. After all, history sometimes shines the spotlight on one character, leaving others in the dark. As such, this book will shed light on the extreme measures taken by Thomas Edison to win the race at all costs, and it will also attempt to give credit where it is due: to Nikola Tesla, a misunderstood scientific genius who cared not as much about the bottom line as he did about sharing his creations with the world.

1 THE CALM BEFORE THE STORM

August 4, 1890, 10:00 p.m.
Auburn Prison, Upstate New York

William Kemmler was a rat in a cage, trapped in an experiment he barely understood. He sat on his cot, staring into the small amount of space around him. A cell does not afford much freedom of movement nor allow a prisoner's gaze to travel beyond the close walls that hold him tight. With bars on one side, brick and concrete on the other three, Kemmler chose brick over iron for his meditation, fixing his eyes on a stained portion of wall that was much like the rest.

Guards appeared often, peering into his cell intently, though not expecting much. The convict had been placed on suicide watch, but he'd never shown any inclination to harm himself. The watch was a matter of routine and had become mandatory as the expected date of execution grew closer. How much closer, Kemmler didn't know. He knew only that sometime between August 3 and August 9 he was to be put to death for the heinous crime he had committed.

■ ■ ■ ■

March 29, 1889, 8:00 a.m.
526 South Division Street, Buffalo, New York

It was neighbor Mary Reid who received the first confession from a blood-drenched William Kemmler, a twenty-eight-year-old vegetable peddler. Staggering into Mrs. Reid's kitchen, the drunk man exclaimed, "I've killed her!"

Reid screamed hysterically, not sure how to take Kemmler's claim. She, like other neighbors, had grown used to hearing violent arguments between William and his wife, Matilda "Tillie" Ziegler. Kemmler was drunk. This was no surprise, even at the early morning hour, but this time he was covered in blood.

Kemmler rushed out of the kitchen and then reappeared moments later with his four-year-old daughter, Ella. The girl cried uncontrollably, splashes of blood on her clothing. Mrs. Reid knew it was true.

A subdued William Kemmler did not resist when taken into custody less than an hour later.

William Kemmler, the first man condemned to death by electricity, *New York Herald*

The crime scene was gruesome. On the hay-covered kitchen floor, in a dark red puddle, was a small hatchet. Twenty-six gashes covered the woman's skull. Five severe fractures highlighted the damage to the woman's head, her right arm had five substantial cuts, and both shoulders had large gashes. Dr. Blackman, the unfortunate gentleman called to inspect the victim at the scene, said it was the worst case he had ever been asked to examine.

At the police station the next day, a hungover William Kemmler was honest with the Buffalo police. "I wanted to kill her," Kemmler admitted. "And I am ready to hang for it."

A moment later, with little more to add, he asked for a glass of whiskey. He was denied.

Kemmler very well might have been ready to die for his crime, but he would not die by hanging. Instead, the only ties that would bind him would be ones that would hold him down. Restraints. Capital punishment had just been turned over to science, and the entire world was talking about this historic news. But Kemmler was illiterate and often intoxicated, so he'd had no clue of the momentous change. A victim of bad timing, William Kemmler—soon to be called a "hatchet fiend" by the press—would be the first to die in the new vehicle of capital punishment: the electric chair.

■ ■ ■ ■

August 5, 1890, 1:00 a.m.
Auburn Prison, Upstate New York

Prison chaplain Horatio Yates and Reverend Dr. Houghton walked close together in the near-empty corridor, not a word uttered between them. They arrived at William Kemmler's dark cell, where the prison guards had to shake the man from sleep.

Kemmler had seen these two men more than a few times over the last several weeks, but a visit in the darkness of night could mean only one thing. The two holy men solemnly informed Kemmler, still prone on his cot, that the time of his execution had been set for 6:00 a.m. the following day, August 6, 1890. Kemmler nodded calmly, turned away, and stared at the brick wall.

It had been a long time coming, and at least, finally, the man who would be the first to die in the electric chair knew when it would all come to an end.

In the morning he'd be set free by the hands of death. It was the most comforting thought he'd ever had. He closed his eyes and fell asleep.

2 THE FIRST SPARK

To start a fire, three crucial elements are needed. There's *heat*, like a bolt of lightning that sparks upon contact and holds the potential for a flame. But a spark alone simply flitters and then harmlessly peters out. So *fuel* is needed to take the spark, hold it, and activate the heat, like cardboard or wood or some other material that—when it interacts and combines with heat—causes a reaction. Add a third element in the form of an *oxidizing agent*, usually oxygen, and the heat and fuel and oxygen mix and combust into a steady blaze.

Fire.

Remove any one of the three elements, and a fire can be avoided or extinguished, like applying water to lower the temperature and disperse the heat. This chain reaction, this fire, can continue to build if the three elements remain in place, as the heat will continue to expand as it comes into contact with more fuel—like a flame jumping from tree to tree in a forest—all the while surrounded by the oxygen in the air.

William Kemmler had become fuel without his knowledge, just another object to feed a fire that had started long before, when three elements had combined to become a combustible force.

■ ■ ■ ■

August 7, 1881, 10:00 p.m.
Brush Electric Company, Ganson Street, Buffalo, New York

George Lemuel Smith was the heat—the first spark that started the fire William Kemmler would help fuel nearly a decade later.

A thirty-year-old dockworker in Buffalo, George L. Smith had just spent another night on the town. Smith was a known alcoholic, and the end of the workday and the setting of the sun usually triggered the call of the saloon for Smith and his buddies. By all accounts, he was a good husband and father, and a strong-bodied man, but prone to temptation and gambling with friends.

Earlier that evening, Smith and three of his friends had reportedly visited the Brush Electric Company plant on Ganson Street. This was not odd; many people from near and far made the visit to Brush Electric.

The plant had been open for a year, built to power the blinding arc lights around the area, which had helped Buffalo develop a reputation as a center of technology and progress. This structure was massive in scale, housing multiple dynamos and generators that held and distributed electric power, which the world wasn't completely familiar—or comfortable—with at the time. To help ease the townsfolk's minds and ensure that this was not a place to be feared, the plant was built with public relations in mind, and visitors were routinely welcomed inside to view the marvel of modern technology.

Just inside the main door, a large generator had become a showpiece for the plant, with many visitors crowding around it during business hours to see the machine at work. As more and more people had come, word had spread that if you held on to the three-foot-high railing that surrounded the generator, you could feel a surge jump from generator to railing to your body. It was a harmless tickling sensation along the skin, one that elicited laughter and smiles in those who experimented with the little game.

Brush Electric security guards and staff did not encourage or promote this activity, but groups of tourists would simply wait until the generator was left unattended. Then these eager visitors would hold hands, trailing the surge harmlessly from the person in contact with the railing to all the others, like an electrified human chain that snaked around the room.

Smith and his three friends had kicked off their night on the town by visiting Brush Electric, holding the railing to experience the surge. But after hitting the saloon and spending hour upon hour downing drink after drink, Smith decided to head back to Brush Electric to "stop the generator," as one of his friends later reported Smith had said.

Smith made his way to the building, but his first attempt was thwarted when the manager of the plant, G. W. Chaffee, chased him off. And the following couple of attempts went much the same way, as other attendants forced him to vacate the premises. But the inebriated man was stubborn and stayed hidden in the darkness, watching and waiting for a final opportunity to make it to the generator.

When Chaffee was forced to look after another generator inside the plant and the police officer and other attendants had walked away from the main door, Smith placed one hand on the side of the generator, expecting the tingling surge he'd felt many times before while holding the railing.

Nothing.

He lowered his other hand to the other side of the generator, sandwiching the powerful monster in a sort of drunken hug. His body went stiff upon contact—his hug giving way to a statuesque pose of an incredibly upright and well-postured man.

The attendants saw Smith's body stiff as a board and quickly rushed to his aid. They tried to pry his body away from the generator but found his hands stuck firmly to the machine, as if a magnetic force had taken hold. Soon after, they had the generator shut down, and Smith's body slumped lifelessly to the ground.

Chaffee and other witnesses claimed Smith had died instantly, no suffering and no cries of pain, and not so much as a small flame or burn left on his body.

An autopsy by Dr. Joseph Fowler in the following days determined Smith had died upon contact with the generator, Fowler officially listing the cause of death as "paralysis of the nerves of respiration." He confirmed there had been no burning skin or tissue damage, supporting witness accounts that no flame or spark had harmed the man's body.

■ ■ ■ ■

Alfred P. Southwick was the fuel—the first source to harness the heat from the spark created by George L. Smith's death.

A dentist by trade, Southwick would not have seemed the most logical person to invent a device that utilized the raw power of electricity. But given the time period, when life was changing quickly and technology advancing by the day, Southwick, like many people of the era, kept his finger on the pulse of the innovative boom around him.

Southwick, a faculty member of the University of Buffalo Dental School, had turned to dentistry later than most, at the age of thirty-six, having been an engineer at the Great Lakes Steamboat Company and then the chief engineer at the Western Transit Company. He published a few scholarly articles on steam engine design and had participated in scientific discussion groups. His experience as an engineer allowed him to experiment with electricity for practical use, and his interest in the science of electrical current continued even after his change in occupation.

As he turned to dentistry, Southwick displayed an inventive mind, designing an effective implant for a cleft palate. He also successfully employed a low-voltage electric current as a numbing agent during oral surgery. His recognition as a leader in the dental field grew.

When Dr. Fowler had presented his findings to a group of

amateur scientists in the days following Smith's autopsy, it didn't take long for the inquisitive dentist to get lost in a whirlwind of wonder after learning that George L. Smith had died instantly by way of the high-voltage exposure, without pain or suffering. Southwick's mind went to work, and he settled on the idea of using electricity as a more humane mode of execution.

The timing was right, as hanging had been attacked as inhumane, with bungled executions piling up and the news sprinkling over the public. New York governor David B. Hill felt the pressure and called on the scientific community to find a more modern method of execution, stating that "the present mode of executing criminals by hanging has come down to us from the dark ages."

Alfred P. Southwick knew he had a better method. But he was a dentist, not a scientist. What ground did he stand on to recommend the use of electricity to replace hanging? He had to be able to show proof that electricity was a more instant, pain-less, and civilized means of death.

The dentist-turned-inventor soon teamed up with Buffalo physician George Fell in designing a device to euthanize animals, namely dogs. In 1887, the two entered into an agreement with the Buffalo SPCA to conduct experiments on stray dogs, which had begun to overwhelm the city of Buffalo to the point where there was a twenty-five-cent bounty on each stray turned in. Southwick and Fell, the SPCA hoped, could supply a humane method of getting rid of the many strays that had to be dealt with.

Their crude design included a "box" filled with an inch of water, with wires from an arc light dipping down into the bottom. Dogs were led inside and, by all accounts, were killed instantly by the high-voltage charge. It wasn't long before Southwick and Fell began designing a chair, modeled after a dentist's chair, to help solve the problem of replacing the "primitive" method of hanging with a more "civilized" mode of execution.

At the same time, Governor Hill was under fire more each day with the continued public fiascos that took place at the gallows. The public was looking to the governor for answers. Governor Hill, who had an eye for the new inventions popping up around the world, claimed science could provide a method that was "less barbarous" than hanging.

Alfred P. Southwick heard Governor Hill's call. He knew this was his opportunity, so he turned to his longtime friend and current state senator, Daniel McMillan. Southwick convinced McMillan to introduce a bill to investigate the "most humane and approved method" of execution. This bill was passed in 1886, and a commission was appointed, originally made up of three men: Alfred P. Southwick himself, Albany lawyer Matthew Hale, and the commodore of the New York Yacht Club, Elbridge T. Gerry. The group was dubbed the Gerry Commission, although it was more often referred to as the "Death Commission."

After studying the history of hanging as a means of execution, the Gerry Commission concluded that there was a definite need for a "speedier and more merciful" mode of execution.

This commission listened to, experimented with, and considered many alternatives, at first leaning toward an overdose of morphine by injection as the top alternative. However, the contentions were that people reacted differently to poisons, with some dying instantly, while others endured a more prolonged death. Additionally, the hypodermic needle was a new device in medicine, and since it was being widely introduced in general practice, physicians did not want the public to develop a negative association for needles. In the end, the Gerry Commission concluded that death by electrocution was the best alternative, as it incorporated the symbol of modernization—electricity—with the need to maintain a civilized society.

The American public, though, balked at Southwick's invention: this "chair of death." The science of electricity, after all, was so new and temperamental. Why trust a dentist, even if he was a member of the "Death Commission"?

The first electric chair, used in 1890, in the execution of William Kemmler

The Gerry Commission wasn't enough to win over the public. Southwick needed an expert to back him and lend credibility to the chair.

He needed Thomas Edison.

■ ■ ■ ■

Thomas Edison was the oxidizing agent—the missing third ingredient needed to create a combustible combination in the form of the functional electric chair.

Just over a decade earlier, Edison had wowed the world with his invention of the phonograph, launching him to instant celebrity status. The man who became known as the father of invention, along with his team of like-minded inventors at his lab in Menlo Park, didn't stop with the phonograph but instead introduced other inventions, including the invention he'd become synonymous with: the light bulb.

An early patent on the design of an incandescent light bulb in 1878 had staved off competitors, but Edison and his team at Menlo Park could not perfect a cost-effective, long-lasting bulb for practical use, despite focusing all efforts on the invention. It wasn't just a bulb that was needed—it was a system of powering it. Finally, two years after the initial bulb prototype and patented design, Edison had designed and mass-produced a long-lasting bulb, one that utilized his own patented system of electric current: direct current.

Direct current (DC) is essentially a one-way street for electricity. The power source, like a battery, gives off power, called electrons, and sends it in one direction. This direction of electron flow is called its circuit. The electricity follows its unidirectional circuit until it reaches the utility, like a light bulb, and it receives power. With direct current, the circuit continues on to the next utility, like an outlet connected to a toaster, and then on to the next utility and then the next. On a large scale, a power generator sends electrons through its circuit to one residence and then the next and the next. The problem with direct current is that the amount of power—the strength of the electrons—weakens the farther away from the power source it gets. Therefore, the farther away a house is from a large generator, the weaker its power will be. This means direct current requires more power sources spaced out from block to block of a big city in order to supply power to everyone. Even so, the residence farthest away, like one on the outskirts of town, would receive less power than those closer to town.

This means direct current was expensive and required a lot of wiring, machinery, and generators that had to be distributed every few city blocks. Costs piled up, and electric light became less for the masses and more for the elite class. Still, parts of New York were lit up by Edison's direct current, and progress was shining down on society.

Competition also surfaced in the form of alternating current (AC), a system that was designed and patented by Nikola Tesla, a former employee of Edison's, and then bought and mass-produced by inventor and businessman George Westinghouse, who became the public figure in direct opposition to Thomas Edison. Alternating current was less expensive and

Thomas Alva Edison

much more aesthetically pleasing than direct current. It required only one large dynamo located on the edge of town, and current traveled back and forth along a single wire.

Alternating current involves a power source, like a generator, that gives off electricity that reverses—or alternates—direction multiple times. This current alternates direction sixty times per second in American AC systems. Alternating current fed through a transformer allows the strength of the electricity to be adjusted, which means the voltage can be tailored specifically for the device being powered. Another key difference between AC and DC is that AC's bidirectional current makes it more suitable for long-distance transmission than DC electricity, so that a residence on the edge of town will receive the same amount of power as one directly next to the power source. This means the AC system needs far fewer power generators than the DC system.

Edison had engaged in battle with his competition, and he was losing in the court of public opinion. Edison was a savvy businessman, and he knew that not just light would rely on the most effective and commercial system of electric current—*everything* would. He was desperate, willing to do anything to prove his system was the logical—and *safe*—choice.

Enter Alfred P. Southwick and the electric chair.

On behalf of the Gerry Commission, Southwick had written to Edison twice to seek advice and his endorsement of the electric chair. At first, these letters went unanswered. Until, finally, Edison ran out of ammunition to fight off his competition.

The electric chair, Edison determined, was the artillery he had been waiting for. In 1888, Thomas Edison endorsed the use of electricity as a more humane method of execution, but only *if* alternating current—since he claimed it was so deadly—was the method of electric current employed. Edison would even recommend that the act of electrocution as capital punishment be termed "being Westinghoused," directly stamping his main competitor's name into the consciousness of the public. Doing so would make it unmistakable that alternating current was a killer—an *instant* killer.

Edison allowed his name to be tied to the creation of the electric chair. It was a bold move. But this man, Edison, had always been a gambler.

3 WHAT'S GOOD FOR THE GOOSE...

Thomas Alva Edison, known as "Al" in his early years, had always possessed a burning sense of curiosity that mixed, often dangerously, with a blind willingness to take risks.

Born on February 11, 1847, in Milan, Ohio—a burgeoning town thanks to the Milan Canal, built to make traveling the twisting, turning Huron River manageable for the many ships carrying wheat—young Al Edison's curiosity nearly killed him a few times over. Like a cat, Al seemed to have nine lives, and his inquisitive, reckless nature did its best to use up each life quickly.

Young Al was amazed at the sights and sounds all around him. And like many children who find themselves confused, Al turned to asking "Why?" and "How?" And ask he did, so much so, in fact, that his father admitted to being embarrassed by his son's silly questions. But when no answers satisfied Al's inquiring mind, the small boy took to personal inspection to find his own answers. Firsthand experience was his solution to the myriad unanswered questions.

Just before he turned five years old, Al was so curious about a grain elevator that he crept closer and closer until he fell in.

Luckily, he was snatched by an alert worker and yanked out of the quicksand-like grain after being submerged for a few moments. If the worker had been a second slower, that lifesaving hand would have been unable to help young Al.

Al also spent some of his nine lives falling into the Milan Canal, like many boys his age had done. But unlike the other boys, who just wanted to get near the water or were carelessly playing too close to the water's edge, what drew Al dangerously close was the canal's construction and practicality, along with the complex and varied ships that used the man-made waterway.

Young Thomas Alva Edison

When he was six, Al noticed a goose resting atop its eggs. The boy pondered the goose's egg-rearing practice and the eventual end result. He desperately wanted to see the eggs hatch, but just as curiosity served as a weakness, so did impatience. If only there was a way to make those eggs hatch sooner. Al became lost in introspection and developed a theory. The next day, Al's mother, Nancy Edison, found him sitting atop the eggs. His mother beckoned him to get off the eggs, grabbed his arm, and pulled him away from the mother goose, who was honking loudly in protest. Mrs. Edison—amused but concerned—asked her son why he was doing such a thing. Al's reply was one of logic. If the heat and mass of the mother goose's rump helped to hatch the eggs, surely a larger rear end—like his own—would expedite the process? Mrs. Edison could only shake her head at her son's naive but intuitive sense of reasoning.

While Al's early inquisitive urges threatened his own well-being, as he grew older they became more dangerous to those around him as well. In the family's final year living in Milan, Al decided he wanted to know how hay burned. *Is it quick-burning? How does it smell? Does the flame jump to neighboring objects once it has used up the hay, or does it peter out and extinguish itself?* He knew asking his father these questions would, as usual, lead to both his father's frustration and an ultimate dead end, so Al decided to light some hay on fire in his father's barn. The blaze grew so quickly and spread so expansively that the barn was a total loss. Al had the answer he'd craved, but it had cost his family dearly in the form of a barn. If that weren't enough, Al was dragged to the village square by his father and publicly whipped as a lesson to him and other youths.

When Al was seven, the family moved to Port Huron, Michigan. The growing and endlessly branching limbs of railroad tracks had expanded to Ohio and the Huron River and had taken over as the primary means of commercial travel. The Milan Canal and the town itself had outlived its usefulness— run over by the modern railway.

Port Huron promised more opportunities for the Edison family and offered Al a chance at a formal education. His public schooling was fleeting, though, and came to an abrupt end a mere three months after it had begun when his teacher Reverend G. B. Engle described Al as "addled" and claimed he was unteachable. Mrs. Edison, having been a teacher in Canada before the family's move to the US, promptly took to homeschooling her son. Nancy Edison recognized her son's unique mind and knew how to tap into and make use of his individual learning style. In fact, an adult Thomas Edison would later conclude about his mother, "If it had not been for her appreciation and her faith in me at a critical time in my experience, I should very likely never have become an inventor."

With his mother's encouragement, Al questioned and experimented. Questioned some more. Experimented some more. It was a way of life for Al, who was growing both physically and intellectually. Around the age of ten, Al became particularly curious about chemistry, his cellar serving as a laboratory. This made perfect sense for young Edison, for although he read widely and enjoyed the process of learning through the written word, he learned early on that "doing the thing itself is what counts." With that in mind,

Al quickly built up a collection of nearly two hundred bottles and containers, which he painstakingly shelved, each labeled "Poison" to scare others from handling his prized ingredients. Mrs. Edison allowed her son to experiment in the cellar but worried about the results and therefore kept a close eye on Al's undertakings. Perhaps the smoke from the burning barn in Milan had followed the family and had not quite lifted high enough to clear the air.

It seemed the older he got, the more Al's curiosity impacted others. Just before his eleventh birthday, Al convinced his childhood acquaintance, a boy by the name of Michael Oates, to do an experiment with Seidlitz, a powdery chemical that turns to gas when mixed with water. Seeing the *powder + water = weightless gas* reaction, Al instructed Oates to ingest a large quantity of Seidlitz, theorizing that the powder would turn to gas when it came into contact with water in the boy's stomach, which in turn would result in the boy floating into the air like a balloon. The Human Balloon Experiment, of course, didn't pan out as Edison had planned. Instead, the failed experiment resulted in a very sick Oates and (after Mrs. Edison had taken a switch to him) a very sore Al Edison.

Experimenting with chemicals also had another consequence: cost. These chemicals and essential ingredients weren't free. If Al wanted to keep up with his experiments, he needed to make money. Eleven-year-old Al Edison soon gained the opportunity to use a horse and wagon to run a relatively large market garden for the Edison family. After doing his share of hoeing corn and working the land, Al would load the wagon with corn, lettuce, and other vegetables to sell to people around town. The enterprise was a success. In fact, Al even took on an employee, Michael Oates, that same boy who had agreed to become the first human-balloon guinea pig. Along with Oates, Al took to business kindly and made a steady profit, though he had no interest in saving any of his money. Instead, every penny was put into his experiments.

With a taste for business but a disdain for physical labor in the hot sun, Al looked around and noticed everything was turning toward the railroad. Grand Trunk Railway was carving its tracks all around him, putting down roots not just in Port Huron and neighboring areas but all over the world. Things were moving quickly. Change was a wildfire. And Al knew he had to hop aboard and go in the direction the world was moving or else he'd risk being left behind.

So at the age of twelve, Al begged his mother to allow him to become a newsboy, selling papers and other goods on the Grand Trunk train that traveled from Port Huron to Detroit. When she said no, he begged some more. She said no again. He begged again. Al was relentless. When Mrs. Edison finally gave in, each day Al traveled the local train's sixty-three-mile route from seven in the morning to nine at night. For the next two years, Al sold newspapers, vegetables, butter, and anything that could help turn a profit. Al also worked as a candy butcher, selling sweets to passengers on the train. During this time, he developed his skills and natural abilities as a salesman and entrepreneur. Making use of his experience with Michael

Oates, Al took on other boys as employees and improved his profits, which, all told, resulted in around eight to ten dollars a day, most of which went directly toward his chemistry obsession; he moved his laboratory from his cellar to an unused baggage-car compartment on the train.

When the Civil War broke out, Al saw the market of the written word become prosperous, especially on the Grand Trunk Railway, so he gave up his vegetable store and focused on the newspaper business. People were hurrying their way through life; spare time was a commodity. The train ride was a small amount of time for passengers to, in whatever way possible, "catch up" with the chaotic world around them. Al sold newspapers as fast as he could acquire them and developed a method of reading and judging the news in advance to decide how many papers to buy and sell.

On April 6, 1862, the Battle of Shiloh had a direct and extreme impact on his business. When Al arrived at the stop in Detroit, a large crowd surrounded the station bulletin board, where a message explained that thousands had been killed and wounded. The savvy newsboy "knew that if the same excitement was attained at various small towns along the road, and especially at Port Huron, the sale of papers would be great." Al moved quickly, working his contacts so that he—with the help of a bribe of free papers for the next three months—talked the telegraph operator into posting the news on the blackboard at each station. This meant that right alongside the arrival and departure times, passengers saw the brief news report teasing them with information about the Battle of Shiloh. Edison then went to the *Detroit Free Press* and convinced them to give him one thousand copies instead of his regular amount of one hundred, even though he didn't have the money to pay for all the papers. Traveling from station to station, he sold the papers quickly. So quickly, in fact, that as the supply dwindled he charged more for each paper, going from the initial amount of five cents up to ten, reaching a pinnacle of twenty-five cents for his last few copies. Business boomed for the young newsboy.

During those negotiating sessions at the *Detroit Free Press*, Al had observed the newspaper trade and had grown fond of it. He had become so enamored that he decided to create his own periodical. Al secured old parts and spare materials from his visits to the offices of the *Detroit Free Press* to make the equipment he needed. He then turned part of his baggage car into a printing press, starting the Grand Trunk's very own *Weekly Herald*, which featured local news and gossip that was written by Al himself. He sold a generous number of what was considered a substantial periodical for three cents a copy, or eight cents for a monthly subscription. He was not even fifteen years old at the time.

Eventually, his mobile laboratory would spell disaster when a shoddy section of track resulted in a jostling train, which ended in a stick of phosphorus falling to the floor and bursting into flames. Al was banished from the train at the next stop by an irate conductor, who Edison claims gave him a severe whack on the side of his head that resulted in his loss of hearing.

Though, in truth, Edison's hearing impairment was present from an early age and got progressively worse over time.

This deafness, regardless of whether it was a direct result of the enraged conductor or had been present at birth, was viewed by Edison as a "great advantage . . . in various ways." He'd attribute his deafness to helping his future success with telegraphy, the vocation of choice that followed his newspaper business, and with his invention of the phonograph later on.

Meanwhile, a constant throughout Edison's childhood and teenage years was reading. He was a regular at the library, and according to Edison himself, "I started with the first book on the bottom shelf and went through the lot, one by one. I didn't read a few books. I read the library." While his father wasn't supportive of his dabbling in chemistry or his new obsession with telegraphy, he did support his son when it came to reading. In fact, he paid Al a penny to read books of "serious literature," starting with Thomas Paine's *Age of Reason.*

Al's laboratory moved back to his cellar, and although his occupational efforts continued with the *Weekly Herald* for a short time afterward, they soon gave way to telegraphy, the long-distance transmission of electromagnetic waves through the air to communicate text and symbols. It was a natural progression for Al, for in his long time on the train as a candy butcher and newsboy, he had become enthralled by the machine shops that peppered the railway stations. He loved the gears in motion, the valves, and the levers that controlled various apparatus, and everything related to the locomotive's design and inner workings.

Along with this machinery, Al noticed that everywhere he went he saw the telegraph at work. This invention, he knew, was something to invest in—both with time and money.

Al the telegrapher was a quick study, and like most of his passions-turned-occupations, the majority of his skill and talent came about by teaching himself through trial and error. But he could only learn so much on his own. He hung around the telegraph office to pick up what he could, but the boy who had a million questions as a toddler had just as many when it came to telegraphy.

Fate intervened and set Al on the path toward his ultimate destiny one day while he was standing among the tracks at a train station. As a boxcar was given a push to move it in the desired direction, a lone boy appeared on the tracks, playing without a care in the world. Al threw down his things and rushed toward the boy, scooped him up, and brought him to safety.

Turns out, the boy was the child of the station telegrapher, James Mackenzie, who had wandered away to receive a message and had lost track of his son. To repay his son's savior, Mackenzie offered to take Al under his wing and teach him professional telegraphy.

Al became addicted with his first lesson from Mackenzie, and after ten days he retreated to his cellar with a collection of equipment and succeeded in building his very own telegraph key, a device that actually sends the telegraph. His years watching the machinists and mechanics around the railway had served him well, and Al became even more dedicated. After five months,

Al had learned enough from Mackenzie to become a professional telegrapher, called a "plug." This classification essentially gave him a badge to work anywhere along the rail line, even though he was only sixteen years old. Al began roaming the country as an itinerant (traveling) operator, taking jobs all over and gaining valuable experience. It was around this time that he decided to drop his childhood name of "Al" and began introducing himself as "Thomas" at each site.

Thomas Edison preferred night shifts for a couple of reasons. First, he had always felt nighttime was the period of greatest concentration, not just for him but for those of the critical-thinking and inventive ilk. And second, he wanted to work night hours to allow himself more time to read, since there was less traffic over the wire, and also to have time to learn about the telegraph itself through inspection and experimentation. This method allowed Edison to advance his knowledge on telegraph technology and electrical science while he worked.

For five years Edison worked all over the country and became a first-rate itinerant telegraph operator. He was chummy with his fellow operators, which was more like a fraternity than a group of coworkers, and he enjoyed the friendly competition and also engaged in being quite the prankster. Things were good for Edison. The problem was: his hearing loss was getting worse with each passing day. Although he considered his deafness a benefit to his work as a telegraph operator because it drowned out the external noises and focused him on the clicks over the wire, his hearing needed to be good enough to pick up even the faintest transmission. His degenerating hearing was making his job more difficult. But, like when he'd saved the young Mackenzie child, fate stepped in and set Edison on the proper course.

After a group of men had seen an advertisement claiming telegraph operators were in demand in Brazil, they chartered a steamer and invited Edison to come with them. Edison abruptly quit his job and set out to join them. Not much is known about why Edison made the decision to leave the country. Perhaps his hearing loss was worse than he had let on. In the end, though, his plans changed when a riot in New Orleans delayed the trip. There, as young Edison waited to continue his trek to another lifestyle, a man told him that only in the US could someone bring out his full worth and achieve greatness. The man continued his commentary by saying any man who believed some other place had a better life in store for him was a "damned fool." Young Thomas Edison left the steamer and returned to Port Huron, the man's voice echoing in his head.

Soon after, Edison moved to Boston, which was considered the center of American science and invention, where he secured a job at the Western Union office, thanks to his close friend Milton Adams, whom Edison had met years prior while working as a telegrapher in Cincinnati. The roaming telegrapher was now stationary for the first time in half a decade, setting up shop in Boston.

It was in Boston that Edison read Michael Faraday's *Experimental Researches in Electricity*. He took in each word wide-eyed, captivated by the principles and theory behind this little-known science. While he wouldn't immediately give himself over to learning about and experimenting with electricity, Faraday's book gave his mind the jolt it needed to focus on not just using technology but improving existing devices and inventing his own.

In 1868, the first in a long line of patents in Edison's name appeared in the form of an automatic vote counter, utilizing a complex mechanical system. It worked well, by all accounts, to the point where recording votes became an easy, accurate task. For this very reason, though, politicians despised the invention, saying they would never use such a device. When Edison gave them a blank stare, he was told, "Young man, if there is any invention on earth that we don't want down here, it is this." These congressmen had the opinion that voting should be slow, drawn-out, and complicated, because they intended to doctor the results in their favor. If a system without any delay or hiccups were set up, there'd be no opportunity to rig elections. "It was a lesson to me," Edison would conclude later in life. From that point on he decided to "never invent anything which was not wanted, or which was not necessary to the community at large."

In the January 1869 issue of the *Journal of the Telegraph*, an announcement read: "Thomas A. Edison, former operator, would hereafter devote his full time to bringing out his inventions." It then referenced an article from the June 1868 issue, in which it had been stated that Edison had created a "mode of transmission both ways on a single wire," which was now, the announcement claimed, for sale at Charles Williams Jr.'s machine shop. Thomas Alva Edison had become the first-ever inventor by trade.

Becoming a full-time inventor was a risky move, one that didn't result in immediate success since his inventions had failed to sell, but Edison decided to double down on his risk-taking and move to the hottest spot for business, invention, and money.

A twenty-two-year-old Thomas Edison arrived in New York broke and jobless. He had a dollar, which he spent on food, and then accepted an offer from friend Franklin L. Pope to hole up on a cot in the battery room of the Gold Indicator Company, where Pope worked. Fate, as it had before, stepped in once again and rerouted Edison's life.

Edison's lucky break involved the stock market, the place where people buy and sell stakes in a business, company, or product. A stock is a share of ownership, and the more units a person has, the more invested they are in the company or product. As more stock is bought, the higher the value of the business or product.

Days after Edison arrived at the Gold Indicator Company, the central transmitter that ran the stock ticker—which displays changes, called "ticks," in the reported up or down movement of a company, business, or product—stopped working. Completely. This ticker was an essential component in knowing the gold prices to help properly advise the Gold Indicator Company's many clients. No one could fix the transmitter, even as bodies accumulated alongside the device and heads were put together. The owner, Dr. Samuel Laws, saw his business crumbling right before his eyes.

Amid the panic, a calm, composed Thomas Edison walked up to Laws and said he could probably fix it if the many frantic workers would clear a path and let him get to it. Laws all but shoved Edison toward the transmitter, the sea of confused experts parting before him.

Edison had spent a good deal of time watching and studying the contraption during his temporary residence in the building. He'd studied its inner workings, so he had an idea what might be wrong. Edison took the cover off the transmitter and picked out a spring that had fallen in with the gears, and it was fixed. The hum of the machinery picked back up, sighs and laughter sprinkled the room, and Thomas Edison was made the chief technical advisor for Dr. Laws.

In this new post, Edison let his gift for making things better shine. From those early days tinkering in his cellar laboratory to selling sweet treats on the rails as a candy butcher to his lesson learned with his creation of the unwanted vote recorder, the young man knew that the key was taking something—whatever it was—and making it more useful to the public. Not because he wanted to better society, but because there was *more profit* in making something more useful.

Edison took this approach at the Gold Indicator Company when he invented a unison correcting device that stopped all stock tickers along a line and reset them at regular intervals. Such a device was direly needed in the industry because mechanical problems happened every so often, with *all* tickers. This resulted in misreading the code on the line, which in turn hurt profits and created a higher likelihood of suffering losses. This correcting device was quickly bought by Gold and Stock Telegraph Company for a lofty forty-thousand-dollar price, which was paid to Edison by check. However, when Edison brought the check to the bank and they claimed it could not be cashed, he angrily went back to Gold and Stock to complain. Marshall Lefferts, the president of Gold and Stock, kindly informed Edison that it was necessary to sign the back of the check to endorse it first. The red-faced inventor nodded and accepted his valuable lesson from Lefferts.

Things picked up in earnest for Edison as he also sold, to Western Union, what would become a widely used device in the form of a type-printing telegraph that would record and print prices of gold and silver.

With another fifteen thousand dollars in his pocket thanks to the sale of the type-print telegraph—after endorsing the check, of course—Edison set up a factory in New York. But that exciting news was quickly followed by sad news from his old home in Port Huron: his mother had passed. His mother's death hit him hard, but Edison had a different way of dealing with grief. He threw himself into his work. With a constantly growing staff of workers by his side, Edison put in long hours and slept sparingly. He was a good boss, most said, the type who didn't ask from his workers what he didn't put forth himself.

In the early 1870s, with his New York factory humming with activity, Edison and company produced a slew of inventions, including a telegraph that printed messages on a strip of paper, and a failed attempt at an underwater telegraphy system for the British post office.

While some inventions flourished and some floundered, Edison's mind-set remained the same: work harder and invent more; learn from failure and use it to improve. One factory grew to three and then four, and never was there a lull in the process, as once an invention had reached a point of stagnation, Edison and his crew directed their efforts to a new project to help maintain consistency without losing productivity.

Finding time to have a family—phrased intentionally, as Edison viewed a wife and children and a home as "things" one should "have," akin to furniture and household supplies—twenty-four-year-old Thomas Edison married sixteen-year-old Mary Stilwell on Christmas Day in 1871. They would go on to have three children together, despite the fact that Edison rarely went home, instead opting to sleep at the factory most days and nights.

Telegraphy remained a focus for Edison, leading to the invention of the quadruplex, a telegraph that sent simultaneous messages over the same wire—something it seemed every inventor was trying to do at the time. Edison also invented and developed the very useful automatic telegraph, which allowed the telegrapher on the receiving end to record the message on a long strip of paper.

Indeed, Thomas Alva Edison had built himself up from the ashes—literally, from the barn fire in Milan, Ohio—but he was not content with remaining where he was. This man had had a taste of success, and he wanted more.

4 A WIZARD IS BORN

While the telegraph served as the springboard device that launched Thomas Edison's career as an inventor, the electric pen was the invention that removed the chains that had held him tightly to the telegraph. It served as an epiphany that there was more to be had in this game of invention, and when it came to profit, he knew, "There is more money in this [invention] than telegraphy."

The idea of the electric pen actually came about because of the printing telegraph, which had left a trail of chemical solution on the paper as it recorded messages. Edison determined that if he could use a small needle to perforate the sheet of paper, it would create a stencil of what had been written. Then the stencil was placed in the press and a roller was used to run ink through the holes in the stencil, which created a copy of the document. It was the earliest form of a copying device and went on to be used for the next century, until the birth of the Xerox machine rendered it obsolete. More important to Edison, this innovation was something different from the telegraph, and it signaled to him that there was an opportunity in inventing on a full-time basis. Thomas Edison the full-time inventor was open for business.

Edison's electric pen

Beginning with about fifteen coworkers—including his dynamic promoter Edward Johnson, chief machinist "Honest" John Kruesi, and right-hand man Charles Batchelor—Edison set up shop in Menlo Park, New Jersey, a place barely listed on the map at the time. Although he was not yet thirty years old, he was often referred to as "the Old Man" by his employees.

Menlo Park became invention headquarters, or as Edison himself called it, his "invention factory." Edison's three-story house was where his wife and children stayed, and it was the first building visitors encountered from the railroad station, which in truth was merely a small wooden platform. In time, a series of other buildings would be added to the surrounding Menlo Park estate. But Edison did not reside in the family house as much as he did in the Menlo Park laboratory. Along with his fraternity of inventors, Edison spent most of his time in the bustling lab.

After a few months getting the building into working order—with a reception room, an office, and a machine shop

Menlo Park laboratory

on the lower level, and the laboratory on the upper floor—Edison and his invention factory began working in earnest in May 1876. Averaging some twenty working hours per day, accompanied by catnaps here and there when he reached exhaustion, the trusted leader of Menlo Park championed his method of producing "a minor invention every ten days and a big thing every six months or so."

And so it went for over a year. Unending work inside the lab, the only downtime the small meals the crew had together, highlighted by the "midnight suppers" they routinely held, which were more about hanging out as a group than a time to have a solid meal.

Minor inventions cropped up, the electric pen continued production, and the automatic telegraph remained a focus. But it was another man's invention that would lead to the invention Edison would later call his "baby."

Alexander Graham Bell invented the telephone in 1876, though many historians argue whether it was Bell or Elisha Gray who truly deserves credit, since initial patents were filed within hours of each other. What would ultimately be considered Bell's creation became a focus for Edison and his group at Menlo Park.

Edison took on the task of trying to improve the telephone—improvement of an existing and successful device sometimes spelled even more profit than the invention itself—and the result was a carbon transmitter that conducted the human voice more impressively than Bell's magnetic model. The creation of his own type of "musical telephone" allowed Edison to enter into competition with Gray and Bell.

It was at the intersection of the musical telephone and the automatic telegraph that Thomas Edison would meet the invention he would later call his "baby," the phonograph. Edison's musical telephone allowed people to hear music even if they weren't where the music was being played. The automatic telegraph made it possible to record a message—with a stylus and a strip of paper—to be read by the operator at a later time. Those two devices were the primary factors that helped conceive Edison's phonograph, as it was a fusion of these two inventions. Along with the electric condenser, which included the idea of applying a coat of wax over paper, these inventions would lead to the birth of not just Edison's "baby" invention, the phonograph, but his status as a full-blown celebrity.

■ ■ ■ ■

July 18, 1877, 12:45 a.m.
Menlo Park, New Jersey

Midnight supper had just wrapped up. Workers were still hanging around comparing different types of diaphragms for the telephone. Without giving it much thought, the Old Man spoke into a diaphragm mounted inside a rubber mouthpiece. He pressed his finger on the other side of the diaphragm as he spoke. The vibrations tickled his fingertips.

"Batch, if we had a point on this," Edison said to Charles Batchelor, "we could make a record on some material which we could afterwards pull under the point, and it would give us speech back."

Edison's statement of observation was a falling domino that pushed its weight into the next, as John Kruesi soldered a needle to the middle of a diaphragm. The next domino fell when Kruesi attached the diaphragm to a stand that held one of the automatic telegraph wheels, which toppled the neighboring domino: Batchelor cutting some strips of wax paper. From there, the line of dominoes fell quickly, culminating with a contraption that had wax paper inserted on top of a wheel, and a needle resting lightly on the paper.

The Old Man sat and lowered his chin to the mouthpiece. As Batchelor tugged the paper, Edison pronounced what had become the standard phrase the lab used to test different diaphragms: "Mary had a little lamb."

Everyone crowded together and looked at the paper, which now held marks on it. Batchelor grinned and placed the paper at the beginning of the wheel, carefully positioning it beneath the stylus. With Batchelor pulling at a steady pace, the needle ran along the marks on the paper.

"Ary ad eh il am."

The place came unglued. Hands were shaken. Backs were clapped and patted. Cheers and shouts sprinkled the room.

"It was not fine talking," Batchelor would later recall, "but the shape of it was there."

A day later—after an all-night, nonstop session that included multiple tweaks and adjustments—the Menlo Park boys celebrated at the next midnight supper after they succeeded in producing a clearly spoken recording.

Although the first public announcement of the invention, which still didn't have an official name, wouldn't happen until a month later, Edward Johnson—Menlo Park's PR man—told the *Philadelphia Record* that the brilliant inventor Thomas Edison had created a device "by which a speech can be recorded while it is being delivered on prepared paper" and then "redeliver[ed]" using the same paper at any time later on.

It would take some time for Edison to present his "baby" to the public in an official manner. In November 1877, Johnson wrote to the editor of *Scientific American* about the invention. Johnson included an engraved illustration to go along with his detailed letter, both showing and telling the general public about the workings of "the apparatus."

Soon after, on December 7, Edison himself brought a newly named phonograph into the offices of *Scientific American* and mystified the editors with a demonstration. Edison later explained: "I . . . set up the machine and recited, 'Mary had a little lamb,' etc. Then I reproduced it so that it could be heard all over the room. They kept me at it until the crowd got so great Mr. Beach [the editor] was afraid the floor would collapse." In the next issue, *Scientific American* recounted for its readers: "The machine inquired as to our health, asked how we liked the phonograph, informed us that *it* was very well, and bid us a cordial good night."

If the term "went viral" had existed in Edison's time, it would have been an apt description for the manner in which news of the phonograph spread across the world. In both Europe and the US, people dreamed about and marveled at the many possible uses of Edison's latest invention. Perhaps remembering the manner in which his automatic vote counter had been slapped down so viciously by the congressmen who had seen it in action, Edison took great care in deciding how best to market and sell this new invention. In late November, the Old Man and his team settled on the idea that the phonograph's greatest commercial potential was as a device for entertainment.

Edison's phonograph launched him into the stratosphere, so much so that he became a household name, synonymous with the idea of science and invention. The man whose formal education had been limited to a measly three months became a renowned scientist. His opinion was sought-after by businessmen, scientists, and writers.

It wasn't just Edison's phonograph that had been born; his reputation and status as a bona fide celebrity had taken form as well. And, having risen so quickly and so monumentally, Thomas Edison had no desire to be pushed down from his comfortable perch atop the mountain. Staying there, he knew, would be a battle.

Journalists came to Menlo Park in droves following the reveal of the phonograph, and Edison welcomed them with open arms. Reporters wanted to know about the amazing phonograph, of course, but they also wanted to know about the intriguing inventor, this Wizard of Menlo Park, as he was later called by reporter William Croffut of the *New York Daily Graphic*.

Amos Cummings, a reporter for the *New York Sun*, visited Menlo Park and chronicled his experience for readers, giving an intimate glimpse of Edison, rounding out edges and defining his image for the many people who were curious. Cummings claimed, "A man of common sense would feel at home with him in a minute." Edison opened up to Cummings and was not shy about his ideas and the grand schemes he had in store. He detailed the many ways the phonograph and related devices he was working on could be used by the public, highlighted by books being recorded and played back, and also how people—parents and politicians, for example—could hide recording devices in critical areas to gain information. Edison seemed to speak on passing ideas that came to mind and mentioned the most incredulous devices and uses, like how he believed an aerophone, a device akin to a megaphone or foghorn on steroids, should be placed inside "the Goddess of Liberty that the Frenchmen are going to put upon Bedloe's Island that would make her talk so loud that she could be heard by every soul on Manhattan Island." Imagine how different a tour of the then-soon-to-be-named Statue of Liberty would be if Edison's idea had come to fruition.

Edison and his team continued to work on a large-scale version of the phonograph and a smaller, more commercial version that would be sold to the public. All the while, everyone wanted a piece of this new celebrity. The *New York Sun* best captured Edison's life: "The people have come to regard him as public property . . . Little knots of people came and went all day long and took possession of him and his office and shop as if they had been personal property."

Thomas Edison needed a break, and his friend George Barker, a professor, talked him into a one-month trip out west. The original intent was to view a solar eclipse from a spot in Wyoming, but the two ended up spending more than the month's time exploring the world they'd only heard of.

⸻

The tail end of 1878 found Edison investing most of his time in his Menlo Park laboratory, along with his staff, focusing on the development of an incandescent light bulb.

Artificial light itself wasn't a foreign concept, as arc lights—two carbon rods set a distance apart and aligned vertically to create a blinding arc of light that bridged the gap between the rods—had been used in variation since 1855. But this form of light was so bright and unattractive that it didn't appeal to most people. The author Robert Louis Stevenson, in fact, described it as "a lamp for a nightmare."

Birds, too, must not have cared for the bright arc light, as it confused them about what time of day it was. They were often heard tweeting and chirping at night when the lights were in use.

The key was harnessing incandescent light—dimmable, controllable lighting—that could be used indoors and for various purposes. No one had done this yet, though many were desperately trying at the time, and Thomas Edison was determined to be the first.

■ ■ ■ ■

September 8, 1878
Workshop of William Wallace, Ansonia, Connecticut

Edison's notion—or better put, his *obsession*—to develop electric light came about on another journey with Barker. While on the trip out west, Barker had asked Edison to visit the workshop of William Wallace and Moses Farmer, who claimed they had designed a machine that powered an arc light system that was called a dynamo, a generator that converts mechanical energy into electrical energy. Edison had shown some interest in electric lighting and agreed. Two weeks after they had returned from their westward trip, Barker and Edison traveled to Wallace's shop in Ansonia, Connecticut, also accompanied by Charles Batchelor and an academic friend of Barker's by the name of Charles Chandler.

A reporter from the *New York Sun* came along to witness the activity. From Edison's first glimpse of the spectacle, the reporter noticed that Edison grew quiet and distanced himself from his companions. As his friends attempted to converse with him, Edison would laugh or nod but then go back deep inside his head. And when he saw the Wallace-Farmer dynamo in use, the reporter wrote, "Mr. Edison was enraptured. . . . Then power was applied . . . and eight electric lights were kept ablaze at one time, each being equal to 4,000 candles . . . This filled up Mr. Edison's cup of joy. He ran from the instrument to the lights, and from the lights back to the instrument. He sprawled over a table with the simplicity of a child, and made all kinds of calculations."

Later, while talking to a reporter from *The Sun* about the trip, Edison declared that he would solve the problem of creating a reliable bulb that was "so simple that a bootblack [a shoeshiner] might understand it." This off-the-cuff statement was merely Edison making a claim in the moment, but it had turned into a guarantee by the "Wizard" himself once it hit print form and was read by the public.

Subdividing the electric light and designing a light bulb wasn't a novel idea. On the contrary, every inventor and scientist, it seemed, was trying to create the perfect incandescent bulb. The host of Edison's visit, William Wallace—along with the absent but equal partner, Moses Farmer—were themselves attempting to make the great discovery. To Edison, this was a chance to one-up every brilliant mind in the world. All these academics and scholars. All these scientists. None of them had been able to invent a practical electric light.

Upon exiting Wallace's workshop, Edison was so confident—so competitive—that he decided to directly address his host. With conviction, Edison said, "Wallace, I believe I can beat you making electric lights. I don't think you are working in the right direction." This wasn't about money. As Edison himself explained in an interview, "I don't care so much about making my fortune, as I do for getting ahead of the other fellows."

Thomas Edison had taken on his most significant competition to date. One he was determined to win, at any cost.

· · · ·

Less than a week after the trip to Wallace's workshop, Edison committed to his promise to deliver by stating he actually had the solution right then and there and only needed "a few days" to put it in practical usage. Perhaps feeling doubters' eyes looking at him from beyond the newspaper, Edison further claimed the "scientific men" were off in their theories, and he predicted that "everybody will wonder why they have never thought of it, it is so simple."

Edison explained his idea of installing small power stations in Lower Manhattan, connecting stations with businesses and houses with insulated wire that would be run underground. These same wires, he theorized, could power any electrical apparatus. When would this happen? "Soon," said Edison.

Having thrown down the gauntlet in the form of a guarantee to have the electric light and its effective system in use "soon," Edison changed his priorities. No longer was the phonograph his focus.

· · · ·

The first issue was designing a bulb, but not just any bulb. One that was functional, and moreover, one that was cheap and able to be manufactured for the masses with profit in mind.

Edison's team began by experimenting with platinum as the filament. Platinum, a silvery-white metal, seemed like a good choice because it had a high melting point and was malleable enough to be bent and coiled easily. The problem with platinum filaments was twofold. First, each platinum filament the team tried only stayed intact for a few minutes because it weakened and broke apart with sustained exposure to heat and oxygen. Even worse, the second problem was that platinum was expensive. Far too expensive to mass-produce for the public, even if it did work for more than five minutes.

Edison had made promises, though, and he had a reputation to live up to. So while he and the others worked on finding a functional and inexpensive filament behind the scenes, in public Edison offered demonstrations to prove he was oh-so-close to producing the genuine article.

One after another after another after another, Edison entertained reporters from four different publications. Each demonstration utilized platinum filaments, and each time Edison kept the bulb lit for less than four minutes, not risking being exposed as a fraud. When asked if he'd encountered any problems, Edison denied complications, even suggesting that the unusual ease with how it was initially progressing was the only unnerving thing. After his final demonstration, Edison played the reporter for the press's full worth, asking the public to remain patient and maintaining that his invention would be available "in good time."

The positive press resulted in skyrocketing interest and financial backing, and Edison Electric Light Company was formed in November 1878.

While Edison continued to entertain the press with stories of how well things were going—never divulging specifics—his "few days" turned into a few weeks, which extended into almost a year. Edison even told the *New York Times* on October 21, 1879, that the "electric light is perfected." It wasn't, of course. Far from it. But an experiment on that day with carbonized sewing thread had resulted in forty hours of illumination without burning out. In truth, Edison's words to the *Times* were more a celebration of *some* progress, when in reality Edison Electric had not gained any ground on finding the answer to the practical incandescent light bulb.

The "success" of the forty-hour burn of cotton thread was something to be excited about. Soon after, though, the cotton filament experienced the same problems. It was not the answer. These many failures, these trials and errors, were not a waste of time to Edison, who would later explain that "many of life's failures are experienced by people who did not realize how close they were to success when they gave up." Edison *was* close.

In the middle of November, the team tried carbonized paper that was bent in the shape of a horseshoe. It lit up the glass globe in a soft shimmer of light as the filament burned.

The team waited.

It still burned.

They waited deep into the night.

It continued to burn.

For over a day the bulb burned. Edison knew he had found the answer. Carbon. "If it will burn for that number of hours now, I know I can make it burn a hundred."

Unlike the bulb experiment, finding the ultimate answer did not happen overnight. Not much ever did in the world of

Thomas Edison posing with his first incandescent bulbs

invention. Instead, Edison led his team on a carbonization quest of every substance they could think of—including fishing line, cardboard, all kinds of paper, and a host of other materials—until, after exhausting over six thousand different options, they determined that carbonized bamboo was the best filament for their incandescent bulb.

It had taken many months of playing the press. Making guarantees and smiling for the cameras. It had been a long journey full of posturing and putting himself in the public spotlight, but maybe now he could get back to what he was born to do: invent. He certainly hoped so. For now, Edison had done it. He'd found success: a simple, inexpensive way to harness light and hold it for a sustained period—safely.

5 AC/DC, A CURRENT CRAZE

It was a man named Edwin Fox, a reporter for the *New York Herald*, who broke the news that Edison had successfully invented and perfected the incandescent light bulb.

Fox, not only a reporter but also Edison's friend, was given access to Edison's lab in the middle of November 1879. For two weeks the reporter had this exclusive access, recording the manner in which Menlo Park was being equipped with some forty bulbs and fixtures. It was a lofty prize Edison had granted to Fox, to be privy to the installation of this new invention, shown multiple demonstrations time after time without any competition from any other reporters, and even walked through in elementary fashion the complicated workings and technical details of the bulb.

The prize had one major condition, though, and that was for Fox to hold off publishing his article until Edison had given him the go-ahead. Edison and his team wanted to go through significant tests, run-throughs, and preparations before Fox let the world know, and Fox, being grateful to have the exclusive dish, obliged and claimed he'd hold off until he'd heard from Edison.

But like the young Thomas Edison, who couldn't wait for those goose eggs to hatch, Edwin Fox simply couldn't put it off any longer. He gave in to his impatience when he published "Edison's Light" in the December 21, 1879, edition of the *New York Herald*.

Fox spared no superlatives in his article, praising the master inventor's "little globe of sunshine" as a perfect device. No gas or smoke or nasty odor. No blinding light to distract the birds. Nor did Fox spare any opportunity to divulge Edison's detailed explanation of the technical workings of the bulb. In the mode of a how-to manual, Fox laid out the manner in which Edison had figured out the elusive mystery many had attempted to solve, spelling out the secrets the Wizard of Menlo Park had shared with him.

Understandably, Edison was at first offended by Fox's betrayal and irritated that his friend had brought the article to press before Edison had given it his blessing. After reading the article again and realizing it was flattering in the extreme as to the inventor's genius, Edison took it in stride and chalked it up as an inevitable occurrence. He knew drive. Competition. Pride. Edwin Fox was much like him, he decided, and Edison followed up the published article with his own version of drive, competition, and pride.

Instead of backing off and slowing things down, Thomas Edison decided it was time to go all in. He'd already made promises and guarantees. He'd claimed he had a bulb that could burn for over one hundred hours and further boasted he could supply a family with light for twenty-four days straight without issues.

How was he to follow up now that Fox had published the details and praised him with such hyperbole? In typical Thomas Edison fashion, with an even stronger and bolder statement: within ten days, he promised, he would light up ten houses in Menlo Park. But that wasn't all. He would also—Edison pledged—set up ten electric streetlamps.

His promises and the tight time constraints he'd leveled on his Menlo Park team were not readily appreciated by his colleagues. But the Old Man was like this, they knew. Sure, they could try to talk some sense into their boss, as one of the company's main investors, Egisto Fabbri, tried to do by asking Edison to first give the lights a test run of a full week before entertaining the ten-houses-of-Menlo experiment. Fabbri's words did very little, though Edison did agree to a four-hour test run on December 27, 1879, which went off without a hitch.

■　■　■　■

December 28, 1879
Menlo Park, New Jersey

No one needed a formal invitation to witness the Menlo Park exhibition. Edison's blanket announcement didn't discriminate as to who could show. As a result, people from all fields of occupation and socioeconomic classes made the trip. This was perfectly fine with Edison, who held claim that any- and everyone should be able to see the light. After all, his bulb was meant for affordable, practical use by all. What better way to drive that point home than by welcoming anyone who was interested?

People came.

And while some of the initial visitors were unreasonably disappointed that the street lampposts were at first not lit up on a real street—and instead were displayed in a bare Menlo Park field—the reaction was positive across the board.

■ ■ ■ ■

The next day, more lampposts were lit along the street, satisfying those hard-to-please early visitors. Within two days, Edison's promise had been fulfilled and ten streetlamps were shining brightly, allowing the growing crowd of visitors—which had quickly soared into the hundreds within a couple of days—to casually stroll along and stop in the laboratory, or at Sarah Jordan's boardinghouse next door, which was fully furnished with lights, or at any of the other buildings lit up on the Menlo Park estate.

Impressed visitors came and went, all paying witness to the spectacle the great Edison had promised. The crowds grew as New Year's Eve neared. What sort of tricks would the Wizard have up his sleeve for the echoing chime of the New Year?

As it turned out, Edison had planned a whole slew of tricks.

A laboratory assistant showed off the way an average bulb would be used in the typical household over a proposed thirty-year span of time, turning it on and off over and over to simulate the many comings and goings of multiple household members. The light never burned out.

A bulb was housed and illuminated underwater in a glass jar, delighting wide-eyed audience members with the shimmering water and shadowy ripples. The Wizard himself was part of the show, just "a simple young man attired in the homeliest manner, using for his explanations not high sounding technical terms, but the plainest and simplest language," as the *New York Herald* described him.

On New Year's Day in 1880, the full weight of Thomas Edison's popularity pressed down on Menlo Park and on the laboratory itself, which was said to have shown signs of significant stress and wear with all the traffic and the beyond-maximum capacity. Inside the lab, light bulbs had been arranged in the shape of a miniature representation of Menlo Park, and this only added to the chaotic pushing and shoving as everyone tried to get a closer look. Hysteria took over, and Edison himself was forced to retreat to his private office in an attempt to quell the commotion his presence caused, like that of a modern-day pop star being clamored after by the public. The white flag was waved the next day when Edison, amid the pleas of his colleagues and business partners, closed Menlo Park to the public.

Now that Edison had the bulb, he knew it was time to take his invention beyond Menlo Park. Everyone around the world deserved to see the light.

One big problem remained: What source of power could be used?

They had invented the light bulb. But that didn't mean anything unless they could develop a system to run it.

■ ■ ■ ■

The light bulb was a brand-new invention. Sure, it was awe-inspiring and a monumental achievement, but housing light in a glass dome was a totally new concept. A host of problems came with inventing something that had no preexisting foundation. If Edison wanted to allow his new bulb to be used by all, that meant he'd have to create everything else to go along with it.

One main issue was that there were no outlets, sockets, or fixtures for this brilliant contraption. In other words, people wouldn't have any way to use the breakthrough device. In modern-day society, if someone gives you a brand-new bulb, you don't look at it with a quizzical expression, wondering how to make it work. You realize you have many options. If you're indoors, you can look around and you'll see a lamp or two, or maybe even five in a room. Or you can find a socket inside or outside any building and simply screw the bulb in, or do a little walk-through and use it with any of the many fixtures readily available. The humor of the saying "How many [insert subject of joke] does it take to screw in a light bulb?" plays on the ease with which the device can be used. *Today*, that is. Not in 1880, when Thomas Edison had just created the bulb and put on a show at Menlo Park.

Even worse, it wasn't only the hardware Edison needed to invent. A whole system of electricity had to be designed and implemented. Wiring, outlets, and power sources and stations. Everything was yet to be created. This system also had to treat the volatile and mysterious science of electricity with the care and caution that was necessary to make it safe for the average person. If inventing the bulb was thought to be difficult, creating a complex and intricate system of electricity was about to make the incandescent bulb look like a child's toy.

▪ ▪ ▪ ▪

Direct current was Edison's first and only love when it came to powering his magical bulbs. That stubborn boy who often refused to accept opinions contrary to his own saw no other manner in which electricity should be conducted and distributed, and at the beginning of 1880 Edison submitted his first patent application for a "System of Electrical Distribution."

There were problems with direct current, especially in the planning stages, as Edison looked to light up New York City, specifically Lower Manhattan. The main problem was that direct current had a short life span in terms of distribution over longer distances (the farther away from the generator/dynamo, the weaker the electric power), which meant multiple large generators and power plants would need to be established every half mile to maintain an even power distribution throughout the city. This meant rural areas were essentially out of luck. For these areas, the solution would be smaller site-based power stations. This was not an initial concern, though, and the Menlo Park boys instead focused on what was needed to power Lower Manhattan, and in the process live up to a promise Edison had made years ago.

Worse yet, the elementary dynamos that existed at the time were not efficient enough to power on the scale Edison needed. These existing dynamos could power the arc lighting systems employed in 1880, but comparing an arc lighting scheme to that of supplying everybody in a given city with light—and powering other devices to come—was laughable. As with sockets and fixtures, here again Thomas Edison knew he'd have to invent something even more important: dynamos that were powerful and efficient enough to do the job.

In addition to the fact that direct current had a short range of distribution, it also required multiple wires. Telegraph and telephone wires already riddled the area like ugly spiderwebs all over environments like New York City, sagging just about everywhere, scaring people who were not at all knowledgeable about electricity. To Edison's credit, he had the foresight to see that adding to the overhead maze would lead to nothing but problems. For this reason, his plan from the very beginning was to bury the wires underground. But this too came with problems, as workers needed to dig ditches all over the city, and the wires themselves had to be insulated.

Edison and his team knew they weren't ready to rush into Lower Manhattan and work out the glitches—the glitches that came with *every* invention, not to mention such a grand one as this. To prepare for the full-scale effort and troubleshoot issues behind the scenes, Menlo Park became a practice field. Wires were laid out in fields around Menlo to represent roads, with some four to five hundred streetlights lining them. Wire was buried underground and insulated experimentally, which would be an early failure and force the crew to spend more time to properly insulate the veins of copper spread through the ground.

Meanwhile, other hungry businessmen and inventors were trying to push Edison from his spot at the head of the table. In October 1880, Edison heard from his old friend and reporter Edwin Fox, who had claimed to witness, out the window of his Manhattan office, a team of workers in the building across the way busily creating bulbs much like Edison's. If this were true, it meant someone else was pushing into Edison's turf.

Edison would later discover that these bulbs were designed by Hiram Maxim and held a signature M-shaped filament, manufactured and sold by the United States Electric Lighting Company. There was no worry in Thomas Edison about someone essentially using his design, as he knew that was inevitable. What worried him was that Maxim and United States Electric were beating him to the punch in the New York City market. This could *not* happen—Manhattan was *his*.

A determined Thomas Edison looked to start his takeover of Lower Manhattan. He hadn't even had a chance to truly explore the details of planning the process before running into a significant snag. His system required power stations with lines running underground to neighboring buildings. *A lot* of lines. To be able to dig and lay the crucial electrical lines, Edison needed permission from the corrupt government of New York City, the New York Board of Aldermen. Edison's idea to win over the aldermen was to throw a massive party that would put his artificial light on display. After an extravagant party and light show featuring over four hundred lamps at Menlo Park in December 1880—with reportedly more glasses of champagne being handled than glass bulbs—Edison got his wish, though the price was still substantial in the end. He'd impressed government officials enough to gain permission to lay the important lines underground where he wanted them, all through Lower Manhattan.

. . . .

Menlo Park had been the perfect place for Thomas Edison and his team of wiz kids to stay relatively close to the action of New York City while maintaining enough separation to stay focused on work. But almost losing Manhattan to Hiram Maxim was too close a call. It taught Edison something very important. If he wanted to light up New York City, he needed to be *in* New York City. Menlo Park might not have been incredibly far from the hustle and bustle of New York City business, but the light from the New Jersey invention factory wasn't bright enough to reach the place he promised to light up. As long as he stayed in Menlo Park, the public would be in the dark about the promise of Edison's light.

Less than a month after the Menlo Park exhibition for the city representatives, Edison Electric Light Company made the bold move of purchasing a four-story brownstone at 65 Fifth Avenue in Manhattan for the specific purpose of being a constant showplace for what Edison Electric had accomplished and what it promised to soon deliver to all.

A gas-powered plant in the basement ran over two hundred Edison bulbs throughout the building, letting the place shine like Manhattan's new North Star, luring people to the open-to-all exhibition. The brass of Edison Electric Light knew it was a genius marketing ploy. But only *if* it came with an ever-present Thomas Edison. They knew the key was to have their prized showman in their Fifth Avenue brownstone.

Many investors were nervous about proposing to Edison the idea of moving him from Menlo Park to the new Manhattan home base, since he had been extremely vocal about wanting to get back to work and turn away from the needy public eye. Some were certain he'd say—or *shout*—no. After all, it wouldn't just mean he'd serve as window dressing, doorman, and glorified tour guide. It also meant turning over operational control of his invention factory to someone else.

Yet, to everyone's surprise, Edison agreed to the move. He was willing to do whatever best helped Edison Electric Light and his precious bulbs.

In January 1881, Edison the inventor once again became Edison the salesman. After a full month of greeting all kinds of visitors—celebrities, scientists, investors, politicians, everyone—Edison brought his family from Menlo Park to Manhattan, housing them in a hotel across the street from the Fifth Avenue brownstone. Within three months, the rest of the workers and equipment followed suit and moved to New York City.

■ ■ ■ ■

Now that New York City was the official home of Edison Electric Light, the real work of setting up a system to power Lower Manhattan began in earnest. The initial task, finding a place to build the first centralized power plant, supplied a reality check for Edison, who initially planned for a single-floor building around two hundred square feet in size. Early efforts included searching in the poorest area, where Edison assumed he could acquire a suitable plot of land and a structure for around ten thousand dollars. Instead, he discovered that none of the buildings were much more than twenty to thirty feet across. And even these properties held a price tag much loftier than the father of invention had anticipated. In the end, Edison settled on two buildings on Pearl Street and paid not $10,000 but an astronomical $155,000. Edison took it in stride. "I was compelled," he explained, "to change my plan and go upward in the air where real estate was cheap." The size limitations forced him to redesign what had called for two hundred square feet by building up instead of across. "I cleared out the building entirely to the walls and built my station of structural ironwork, running it up high."

For the next two years, Edison would expand his business and work on making Pearl Street the power plant it needed to be. His business enterprise grew as he took on Edison Machine Works—housed in a separate building on the Lower East Side—to design and manufacture his dynamos, which had to be built completely from scratch to support the power needed. When the Edison Electric board of directors didn't wish to get involved with manufacturing light bulbs, Edison and a few of his closest colleagues, including Charles Batchelor, created Edison Lamp Company. Indeed, Edison had gone all in with his plans to deliver electric light to the world.

Edison Machine Works

At the same time—less than half a year from the Menlo Park exhibition for the champagne-infused politicians—upward of four thousand applications for on-site "isolated" plants came rolling in. These consisted of small generating plants for the lighting of individual homes, factories, and businesses. Initially, Edison denied these requests and focused solely on his promise to light Lower Manhattan. Once he'd accomplished that, he would tend to the rest of New York City. By November 1881, though, Edison had been convinced to allow some applications to be approved, and the Edison Company for Isolated Lighting was established. Isolated plants were installed and accepted gratefully in various locations around the world, totaling over two hundred by May 1882.

Back in New York City, the process of lighting and powering Lower Manhattan dragged on. By the end of 1881, only a third of the district had been wired. It was clear this was going to take time.

Finally, on September 4, 1882, at 3:00 p.m.—four grueling years after Thomas Edison had announced his first news about the electric light—a switch was thrown, amid much pomp and circumstance, and Edison's bulbs spread light around Lower Manhattan. As a reward to the first customers, the first four months of lighting were free of charge.

For two years the output of Pearl Street, along with the number of customers, slowly grew. But not without issue. All this high-powered machinery and all these devices were new—literally, they had just been created out of nothing—and problems developed.

To help solve the problems that cropped up, Edison, as he always did, turned to his trusted team, which had expanded like his business. In 1884, one new employee would have a brief tenure with Edison Electric but would linger like a thorn in Edison's side for years to come.

. . . .

Nikola Tesla was a Serbian immigrant brand-new to Edison Electric, and he was hungry to show his boss what he could do.

It didn't take long for Thomas Edison to notice both Tesla's eagerness and skill, so to test the new guy, he challenged him to fix the issues with Edison's lighting system aboard the SS *Oregon*, which was docked in the East River, unable to make its voyage.

Tesla worked an all-nighter aboard the *Oregon*, determined to stay aboard until he had met Edison's challenge.

The next morning at five a.m., Tesla saw Edison and Charles Batchelor walking toward him on Fifth Avenue. As Tesla recounted the experience: "When I told [Edison] I was coming from the *Oregon* and had repaired both machines, he looked at me in silence and walked away without another word. But when he had gone some distance I heard him remark, 'Batchellor [sic], this is a good . . . man.'"

Edison and his original dynamo

Nikola Tesla had shown up at a time of growth, commotion, and difficulty for Edison Electric. The company was taking on customers, adding buildings and institutions, and branching out. This, of course, meant more central stations were needed, and more power from their dynamos.

After Tesla had shown his worth, he waited for the right time to tell his boss he had a safe way to power many more homes and buildings with far less physical material expended. Alternating current, Tesla was certain, was the answer. It's unclear when, exactly, Tesla had this conversation with Edison, as it varies from source to source. But gleaned from multiple sources, it's clear Tesla did at one point hold an audience with Edison, during which he explained the many benefits of alternating current. These benefits included needing fewer power stations (one on the outskirts of town as opposed to needing one every half-mile with direct current), using less wire, and having much more power that could be distributed as seen fit, not just for lights but for any and every other electric device.

Edison seemed not at all interested, and it's not clear how much of a chance Tesla had to discuss his scheme with his boss. According to Tesla, Edison was resolute that he had no intentions of even entertaining the notion of employing alternating current. Tesla explained that Edison claimed "there was no future to it and anyone who dabbled in that field was wasting his time; and besides, it was a deadly current whereas direct current was safe."

Instead of theorizing over a deadly science like alternating current, Edison had another challenge for Tesla. He told him to work on the system they were using—direct current—and improve the dynamos and the efficiency of the system. According to Tesla, Edison had "promised me fifty thousand dollars on the completion of this task."

Nikola Tesla believed strongly in alternating current, but he also loved a challenge. Fifty thousand dollars was nice, too, so he committed himself the same way he had aboard the *Oregon* and "designed twenty-four different types of standard machines with short cores and of uniform pattern which replaced the old ones." After several months, he had done it. Tesla had essentially tripled the output of a system he didn't even believe was as efficient as the one he had designed, and he'd done so for his boss. It was time to collect on the promise Edison had made.

Upon completion of his work, Tesla approached Edison and detailed the work he'd done. Then he inquired about the fifty thousand dollars Edison had promised. Edison shook his head. "Tesla, you don't understand our American humor. When you become a full-fledged American, you will appreciate an American joke."

Edison was right: Tesla didn't understand the humor in this supposed joke, and he didn't understand this man's method of doing business, either. Moreover, he also didn't understand why this man was foolish enough to stick with a system of current that was clearly inferior to his.

Tesla had had it. He'd learned a tough lesson about business, about trust, and about Edison. "This gave me a painful shock and I resigned my position." With no monetary gain realized for his hard work and ingenuity, Tesla's short tenure with Thomas Edison was over less than a year after it had started.

Just like he had been a year prior when he'd first arrived in America, Nikola Tesla was on his own. Yet in truth, this wasn't unusual for him. He'd learned early in life that being alone is the price often paid for being unique.

And this man—Nikola Tesla—was nothing if not unique.

6 FLASHES OF LIGHT

lthough his birth certificate lists July 10, 1856, as the day Nikola Tesla was introduced to the world, the man himself vehemently claimed he was born on the very moment of transference from one day to the next, at the "stroke of midnight" where July 9 and July 10 intersect.

True, July 10 has been noted as Nikola Tesla's birthday ever since, but it would only be fitting if Tesla actually *was* born at the exact moment where two days changed hands. After all, where does one place a man born in between two days? Should the recorded date of birth list *two* dates? Or does this defy what a birth*day* actually is? If it were to be decided—by the people who decide such things—that this rare occurrence necessitated two dates to be listed, would the man then have *two* birthdays and not one? And further, if two dates were to be listed, how could it be explained to people in later times that a man had been born on two different days? These questions and their perplexing, cyclical nature mirror the man who claimed to own the rare birthday. Nikola Tesla simply didn't fit within the world's defined parameters, beginning from his earliest moment of existence.

Tesla's birth wasn't just odd in terms of the hands' position on the clock, but in terms of the weather as well, as a raging electrical storm had manifested over Tesla's family home, located in what is now Smiljan, Croatia. The tempest rained down crackling shafts of light and meteoric drops of water in equal measure. The family's midwife, noticing the omen of the boy's birth at midnight, made the assertion that Tesla was a "child of the storm," meaning he'd be a cursed child "of darkness." Nikola's mother, Djuka Mandic, quickly corrected her. "No," she said flatly. "He will be a child of the light." She had no way of knowing how accurate that premonition would become.

Nikola's mother was a descendant of one of the oldest and most traditional Serbian families, a "line of inventors" who had "originated numerous implements for household, agricultural and other uses." Tesla—called "Niko" as a young boy—recognized from an early age that his mother "worked indefatigably, from break of day till late at night," and she was "an inventor of the first order," who "invented and constructed all kinds of tools and devices and wove the finest designs from thread which was spun by her."

Young Niko's childhood involved creating devices useful to him at the time. Contraptions like a cornstalk popgun and fishing hooks for catching frogs offered him some entertainment in his early years. A rather clever invention Niko developed as a boy was the four-bladed wooden propeller to whose blades he attached, by way of adhesive or threaded restraints, three or four

May-bugs each. These rather bulky, powerful-but-clumsy flying bugs "were remarkably efficient," according to Tesla, and he noted that "once they were started they had no sense to stop and continued whirling for hours and hours." It was a source of much amusement for young Niko, until a neighborhood boy decided to put an end to the whirling dervish by eating the bugs. The hideous sight "terminated my endeavors in this promising field and I have never since been able to touch a May-bug or any other insect for that matter."

While Nikola's mother supplied him with an inventive and hardworking example, his father, Milutin Tesla, was an Orthodox priest. But Niko didn't gain a strong sense of faith from his father, as the boy never could devote himself to the spiritual calling he was supposed to follow. Instead, Niko gained other training from his father, who was also a writer. "The training he gave me," an adult Nikola would later comment, "must have been helpful. It comprised all sorts of exercises—as, guessing one another's thoughts, discovering the defects of some form or expression, repeating long sentences or performing mental calculations. These daily lessons were intended to strengthen memory and reason and especially to develop the critical sense." Milutin was not without his peculiar features and mannerisms. The man was prone to talking to himself, often using different tones and accents, which an adult Nikola Tesla would also do later in his own life.

In the time period in which Nikola was born, boys in his country had two options from which to choose as a future:

one was the army, and the other was the clergy. Naturally, Nikola was expected to follow his father's lead. Niko didn't care for either option but felt compelled to hold the path his father had blazed for him, especially given the fact that the family had experienced tragedy with the loss of Niko's big brother, Dane, who an older Nikola described as "gifted to an extraordinary degree." Dane's death, an accident with the family horse, had left his parents "disconsolate." After Dane's death, Niko felt that anything he did "that was creditable merely caused my parents to feel their loss more keenly." Certainly, he felt the added pressure that he should continue the family legacy and join the clergy.

Niko experienced what some have referred to as "hallucinations" and others as "visions" and still others would claim were "out-of-body experiences." As Tesla himself described, "I suffered from a peculiar affliction due to the appearance of images, often accompanied by strong flashes of light, which marred the sight of real objects and interfered with my thought and action." He'd go on to explain that these images were of things he had actually seen, not imagined apparitions, though it became difficult at times to decipher what was real and what was not. To help heal himself, Tesla turned to the power of the mind, fully focusing his train of thought on something else. This often worked, but it wasn't as effective once he'd exhausted the images he had actually seen. Imagination then intervened and morphed with reality, forcing his mind to focus even harder. In time, his mind would take him on "journeys—see new places, cities and countries—live there, meet people and make friendships and acquaintances and, however unbelievable, it is a fact that they were just as dear to me as those in actual life."

Niko's time attending Real Gymnasium—middle school to those in America—was hindered by these flashes, though the boy showed early signs of a brilliant mind. Niko read every book he could find about electricity and "experimented with batteries and induction coils." Indeed, Niko's intellect was advanced, further evidenced by the fact that calculus, often seen as a labyrinth to most students, was so simple for Niko that his teachers accused him of cheating.

Social settings and relationships of all kinds were not as simplistic as calculus, and certainly not as appealing as learning about electricity. Niko's labyrinth was dealing with his peers, which is why he often preferred the company of birds and other animals over people.

One experience that perfectly captures Niko's lack of social tact involved two of his old aunts—both unattractive to the extreme, according to Tesla. After going back and forth about their appearance, the two aunts asked Niko to settle the argument and tell them who the more attractive aunt was. As Tesla explained, "After examining their faces intently, I answered thoughtfully, pointing to one of them, 'This here is not as ugly as the other.'"

Naturally, childhood was difficult for a boy who suffered from "flashes of light" and social anxiety. He "had many strange likes, dislikes and habits." One item he held an extreme disdain for was earrings, especially pearls, which would put him into hysterics on sight. Touching another person's hair caused Nikola to convulse and shake as well. And peaches—nothing disgusted him more than the spherical, fuzzy fruit. Yet shiny objects, like diamonds or crystals, pleased him very much, as did objects with "sharp edges and plane surfaces." Birds fascinated Niko, to the point where he'd spend hours playing with the local birds on the farm like he was playing with a group of friends. Niko also *had* to have everything arranged in neat, logical order and sequence, and it was imperative that routines be repeated in exact replication each time. A psychiatrist today might classify this as obsessive-compulsive disorder, but in Tesla's time he was just labeled "odd," the same label he'd earned due to his visions.

Much later in his adolescence, when he was seventeen, these flashes became productive. In his mind, seemingly before his eyes, he gained visions of his inventions. A device and its workings would manifest in great detail, making it so the physical creation was all that was left. No theory or tinkering was needed. His mind—these visions—had shown him what to do. "When I get an idea," Tesla offered, "I start at once building it up in my imagination. I change the construction, make improvements and operate the device in my mind. . . . In this way I am able to rapidly develop and perfect a conception without touching anything."

During his early teen years, one of Tesla's most detailed visions was of a place he had seen in the books at school: a place called Niagara Falls. These falls, beautifully depicted in illustrations and drawings, along with detailed text descriptions, were a miraculous natural phenomenon to Tesla. As he saw the falls more and more and let the images capture his mind, a flashing vision came to him, one that involved a giant wheel being turned continually by the powerful, roaring waves. Later, he vowed to his uncle that one day he would travel to America and see this scheme realized. This vision of Niagara remained in his consciousness—with as much detail as the day it had appeared—for the rest of his life, calling him toward it on an almost daily basis.

Nikola's late teen years resulted in vices, including smoking and gambling. To Nikola's father, a man of little vice and plenty of virtue, this was unacceptable. But to his mother, a woman who had come to understand the nature of man—having surrounded herself with stubborn, willful men earlier in life—it was merely a matter of experimenting, learning, and changing. To this end, she once gave her son a lofty sum of money and told him to go and spend it all. Nikola did just that, and blew through the lot so quickly that he felt guilt and, according to Tesla, "only regretted that [my addiction] had not been a hundred times as strong. I not only vanquished but tore it from my heart so as not to leave even a trace of desire." Tesla applied his strong mind to fixing his smoking habit and his predilection for drinking too much coffee, and in essence willed his vices away for good.

At the age of seventeen, Nikola was set to join the clergy, but

The charismatic and enigmatic Nikola Tesla

not of his own accord. His father, and everyone around him, didn't entertain any other choice for a future. Then fate intervened in the form of a severe case of cholera, which held Nikola at death's door. In bed and seemingly ready to die, he said something to his father, musing that if he would be promised the chance to go to school and study electricity, then perhaps he would get better. Upon his father's vow, Tesla miraculously recovered.

Nikola Tesla's higher education began in 1877 at the age of twenty-one. He attended Realschule, Karlstadt in Germany, where he dove headfirst—*mind* first—into the study of electricity. It fascinated Tesla. Everything about it.

Now as a young adult with ample education and a developed mind, these flashes of light turned into flashes of brilliance, both in the form of light and the form of grand schemes. His professors, though, were not appreciative of Tesla's constant challenging of the curriculum. While they talked about the functionality of direct current and its safe and productive nature, Tesla argued that it was an incredible waste of energy. He believed it to be a system of electricity that would only hit dead ends. To Tesla, alternating current was the answer, one that had no dead ends and only kept going due to its logical scientific principles.

In 1880, Tesla finished his studies by attending lectures at the University of Prague, but he never graduated with a degree. Tesla then transitioned from the classroom to the workplace, taking a position at the Central Telegraph Office in Budapest in January 1881. While in Budapest, alternating current dominated his every thought, and time working on his alternating current motor consumed him. This predisposition to light and electricity can be traced back to two related boyhood experiences, both of which included Niko's favorite childhood companion, the family cat, Macak.

One dry winter day, Niko brushed his hand along Macak's back. "I saw a miracle that made me speechless with amazement. Macak's back was a sheet of light and my hand produced a shower of sparks loud enough to be heard all over the house." These sparks were the beginning, the heat to start a lifelong blaze in Tesla's mind. The other experience, not long after the first, happened when Macak sauntered across a cold, dark room in the candlelight. Tesla's memory held that image for many years. "[Macak] shook his paws as though he were treading on wet ground. I looked at him attentively . . . surrounded by a halo like . . . a saint!" These two experiences together kept Nikola Tesla asking every day, "What is electricity?"

When Tesla was twenty-six, a different experience would mix with the two childhood memories with the family cat and serve as a compass to guide the rest of his life. It happened in Budapest, during a walk with his college friend Anthony Szigeti, when a severe vision came to him, one that held great clarity like no previous flash of light. Tesla observed a host of circular objects around him and the vision grew more finite and tangible. His vision was a round object full of energy, reminiscent of the sun. Fixed in four different spots—like the twelve, three, six, and nine on a clock—hard coil wrapped around the edges of the circle. This round orb of energy spun from one station of coil to the next, as if one coil was activating and then deactivating, and then the next, and then next, until the circle was continually pulled around and around without any noticeable end. It was a vision that would change not just more of Tesla's thoughts but also the history of humankind. Tesla had just "seen" his alternating current motor at work. He had invented an alternating current induction motor.

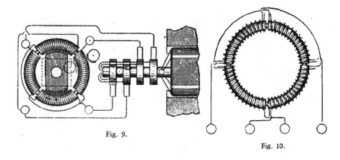

Fig. 9.

Fig. 10.

Schematic of Tesla's alternating current motor

Of course, now that he'd invented it in his mind, he had to physically construct the motor. So from 1880 to 1884, Nikola Tesla worked on his motor, trying to make it function just as it had when he'd envisioned it. During this time, he desperately tried to get backing to produce his motor in Germany and in France, but he never came close to success in gaining investors.

Then, in 1884, while Edison Electric Light was installing a direct current system in Paris, Nikola Tesla came across a man named Charles Batchelor, who just so happened to be Thomas Edison's trusty right-hand man. Batchelor was running the Edison plant in Paris while Edison himself was getting things in order back in New York. Tesla's work attracted Batchelor, who soon offered to write a letter for the Serbian inventor. Later, Edison would mistakenly refer to Tesla as the "Parisian" because Batchelor had told him they'd met in Paris.

Tesla knew that if anyone could help him develop and produce his alternating current motor, it was the father of invention, Thomas Edison. This was Nikola Tesla's big break.

A long journey was in store for the twenty-eight-year-old Tesla. The eager inventor boarded a ship and took off on an arduous seafaring adventure. With only four cents in his pocket, he touched American soil in New York City on June 6, 1884, with a recommendation letter in hand from Charles Batchelor addressed to Thomas Edison. Tesla opened the letter again. Like he had many times aboard the ship, he ran his eyes over the part that made him certain this was meant to be. "I know two great men and you are one of them," Batchelor had written to Edison. "The other is this young man."

Tesla hurried off to find his destination, a place on Fifth Avenue, where the great Thomas Edison was said to be. As he walked, Tesla's flashes of light spread before him, all filled with this great man, the one and only Thomas Edison, falling in love with his alternating current motor.

7 WHAT'S MINE IS YOURS

After leaving Edison Electric, Nikola Tesla might have been alone and exposed to the harsh conditions of unemployment—broke and in need of direction—but the Serbian immigrant had learned some valuable lessons during his time under Edison's umbrella.

First, Tesla learned that his competition, even the vaunted Thomas Edison, was not without vulnerability. The fact that he could improve Edison's production and machinery showed Tesla he was a step above his competitors when it came to intelligence. Further, the manner in which Edison shunned all discussion of alternating current told Tesla that the master inventor was nervous—afraid someone would come along and best his prized direct current approach. Tesla was certain that his design was more advanced and more practical than direct current.

The problem, Tesla had discovered, was the fact that this man was "the" Thomas Edison. He'd proven himself. "I was amazed at this wonderful man who, without early advantages and scientific training, had accomplished so much," Tesla concluded. In contrast to the Serb's extensive education, Edison had scant formal training, yet he was still as bright as the bulbs he'd invented. Edison wasn't just smart in innovation; the man known as the father of invention was wise when it came to knowing how the world worked. How business worked. How *people* worked.

Even with newfound confidence that he was up to the challenge, Tesla found himself without many scientific or business contacts. And more important, he lacked financial backers. But in March 1885, Lemuel Serrell—a former agent of Thomas Edison's—along with patent artist Raphael Netter, stepped in and gave Tesla the guidance he needed.

Serrell understood the extent of Tesla's brilliant mind, and he took the time to break down the business side of the invention process, allowing Tesla to understand the important concept of making fragmented improvements to already established inventions, in order to prove his skill set. In return, Tesla paid Serrell and Netter for their services.

But working on another person's invention was relatively foreign to Tesla, as he had always spent his time creating extravagant inventions in his head, like building unique worlds piece by piece with his imagination until everything was functional in his mind. He had never considered looking at the flaws of existing inventions and modifying them with an eye on patenting the improvements. It took Serrell's insight and tutelage to show Tesla that there was money to be made by improving existing inventions. And more important for the unproven immigrant, patenting these improvements would help him build a name for himself.

On March 30, 1885, Serrell and Netter helped Tesla patent his first improvement of an existing device by eliminating the flickering that often made arc lights a crackling nuisance. Not long after, in May and June of that year, two more patents were issued, including an improvement to the dynamo commutator to prevent sparking. In July, a fourth patent was added to his collection, making four patents in a mere four months.

This work did exactly what Tesla had hoped; it helped him gain business contacts, two of whom would soon become both a blessing and a curse. During his meetings with Serrell and Netter, Nikola Tesla met Robert Lane and B. A. Vail, two New Jersey businessmen who saw potential in the young inventor. To Lane and Vail, Tesla was a magnificent pearl that had been hidden from view; here was a man who had proven he could make technology more practical, and no one had yet cracked the shell to see the brilliance inside. Now that Lane and Vail had discovered Tesla, they were determined to cash in on their find.

Tesla's mind was in perpetual motion, inventions constantly assembling themselves in his overactive brain, and these two men were there to supply the capital that would allow these visions to be brought to life. In exchange for their capital investment, Lane and Vail would hold control of the patents and the company itself. Impulsively, Tesla agreed to partner with these two businessmen, and Tesla Electric Light and Manufacturing was established in Vail's hometown of Rahway, New Jersey. But before they got to Tesla's alternating current system, Lane and Vail made Tesla promise to commit himself to the Rahway project.

With vague assurances that the company would soon begin work on Tesla's alternating current system, Tesla began working on a solitary project for the good part of a year's time: designing, developing, and implementing the first and only municipal arc lighting system in the town and factories of Rahway. Although his alternating current visions would continue to dominate his mind, Tesla went at the Rahway arc lighting project with tenacity, drawing the attention of George Worthington, the editor of the renowned *Electrical Review* journal, who featured Tesla's system on the front page of the August 14, 1886, issue.

In turn, over the following months Tesla and his partners advertised the company's work in the publication, hiring a mechanical artist from New York City to draw the lamp and dynamo, while Tesla wrote copy that claimed theirs was "the most perfect" and "entirely new" arc lighting system. The company, and more important, the Tesla name, was getting noticed.

Unfortunately, after the work on the Rahway project had been exhausted and Tesla broached the subject of working on alternating current—as his partners had promised—it became clear that Vail and Lane had no desire to invest in what they had determined was a "useless" invention like AC. Tesla was outraged, having doubled his efforts with the Rahway project for the sole purpose of expediting the process and getting to work on his AC plans sooner.

To Vail and Lane, though, the company had done all they had envisioned, and they dealt Tesla the "hardest blow I ever received" when they forced him out of his own company with "no other possession than a beautifully engraved certificate of stock of hypothetical value." Like Edison had done to him more than a year earlier, Vail and Lane had duped Tesla out of any material gain for his hard work.

■　■　■　■

The winter of 1886–87 found Tesla taking various service jobs repairing electrical equipment, followed by a period of digging ditches for Western Union's underground cables. While his extensive education and training went to waste, Tesla endured what he would call his season of "terrible headaches and bitter tears, my suffering being intensified by my material want."

Despite this difficult time in his life, Tesla did manage to file a patent for a new kind of motor that utilized the relationship between heat—and the lack of it—to produce and remove a magnetic force. This notion had been inspired by something Tesla had learned during his disappointing tenure under Thomas Edison.

It had become known internally at Edison Electric that an 1884 experiment using coal to heat and power electricity had resulted in the coal overheating and eventually culminated with the production of a gas that ignited and caused an explosion so powerful it blew out the windows of the laboratory. Tesla, upon hearing the many tellings and retellings of the story, got lost in the science of the accident. He knew that heat forced a loss of magnetic attraction, and conversely when cooled reintroduced the magnetic force, only to be lost again when back in contact with heat. If, he determined, this cyclical pattern could be harnessed and maintained, it could cause a continuance of movement, with the end result being a rather effective motor. Thus, his thermomagnetic motor was contrived and then patented, all while he toiled in the ditches he was digging for Western Union. It was reminiscent of his miraculous birth during a violent storm; some good always seemed to come with the bad for Tesla. Such would be the case with his ditch-digging work.

Tesla had explained his thermomagnetic motor to the foreman of his crew, who in turn notified the superintendent of Western Union, Alfred S. Brown, about the invention. Brown, who had previously read about Tesla in the *Electrical Review* feature, decided he needed to meet with this genius scientist who was wasting his brilliance digging ditches.

Brown knew the limitations of direct current, and he swiftly contacted his friend Charles F. Peck, a distinguished lawyer, to see if he wanted to partner with Tesla. Peck had vast knowledge of patents along with ample business sense, and he also had a good deal of capital to offer. The problem, Tesla learned, was that Peck believed alternating current to be a waste of time, so much so that he declined Tesla's invitation to witness his AC tests and demonstrations. Tesla needed to win this man over, and he needed to do it with flair.

"Do you remember the 'Egg of Columbus'?" Tesla asked Peck when he'd finally gained an audience with him.

Peck nodded, acknowledging that he knew of the myth.

Christopher Columbus, as the story goes, had also met with

disbelievers about his theories and his desire to explore the far reaches of the sea. As a challenge, Columbus allegedly asked his doubters to balance a hard-boiled egg on its end, which of course led to many failed attempts and frustrations. Columbus then offered a wager: If he could balance an egg on its end, would they grant him an audience with Queen Isabella? They laughed and agreed, certain that if *they* couldn't do it, there was no way this man would be able to. Columbus, with no hesitation, struck a gentle blow on the end of an egg and cracked its shell, and with little effort placed the egg on its end. He had balanced the egg just as he'd claimed he would. His disbelievers were impressed with the man's fresh way of thinking and ingenuity, and soon after Columbus had his meeting with Queen Isabella. The rest, of course, is history, as Columbus was given the ships and funding for his journey to the Indies.

Noticing Peck was not amused or intrigued by his allusion, Tesla quickly added that he'd do it "without cracking the shell." Peck's eyes glimmered, so Tesla went in for the kill. "If I should do this, would you admit that I had gone Columbus one better?"

When Peck agreed that doing so would impress him enough to gain his support, Tesla dashed away and secured a hard-boiled egg. He headed to a local blacksmith, who fashioned a copper plating for the egg, several brass balls, and pivoted iron discs. Next, Tesla constructed a circular wooden enclosure with polyphase circuits along the perimeter and headed back to see Peck and show him how he could go "one better" than Christopher Columbus.

With confidence, Tesla placed the egg in the center of the enclosure and turned on the current. The egg spun, at first with an awkward wobble. Then the speed picked up and the egg righted itself and spun on its end. Tesla looked at Peck and grinned. He had balanced the egg on its end . . . *without* cracking the shell. Even better, he had also demonstrated the fundamental principles of alternating current with this rotation of a magnetic field.

Reproduction of Tesla's "Egg of Columbus" display

Handshakes were exchanged, and Tesla, Brown, and Peck formed Tesla Electric Company. They agreed to split the patents fifty-fifty, and then structured their deal so profits and resources were split with a third going to Tesla, a third to Brown and Peck, and the remaining third being invested in future inventions.

This last component helped to calm Tesla's apprehension about going into business with others, especially after his horrible experiences with Edison, Vail, and Lane. An additional salary of two hundred and fifty dollars per month further assured Tesla that Brown and Peck were investing in a long-term future with him—one that would focus on his obsession: alternating current.

∎ ∎ ∎ ∎

In April 1887, Tesla Electric Company opened for business in the upper level of a building at 89 Liberty Street in New York City, which was adjacent to what is today the World Trade Center. The lab was scant, with merely a workbench, stove, and a Weston dynamo as furnishings.

Nikola Tesla

On the lower level, Globe Stationery & Printing Company ran a steam engine during the daytime, a fact that benefited Tesla. Brown and Peck took advantage of this by utilizing the steam engine for power at night, converting Tesla—like his rival Thomas Edison—into a night-owl worker, a habit that would extend throughout the rest of his life.

Brown and Peck had complete confidence in Tesla's alternating current system, and Tesla was able to quell his paranoia and distrust for business partners as the relationship proved to be one of mutual respect and trust. Because of this, Tesla agreed to work on other inventions while developing alternating current.

With Peck handling most of the patent business and supplying the bulk of the capital and Brown serving as a technical expert, the three partners became such a good team that it took less than a year for Tesla to design three complete systems of AC machinery (single-, two-, and three-phase currents), produce dynamos for all three phases, construct motors for producing power from the dynamos, and put together transformers for automatic control of the machinery. Tesla calculated the complex math behind his inventions, allowing Peck to file detailed patents.

Tesla Electric Company was well on its way, and the name Nikola Tesla was slowly starting to cross the lips of more people in the fields of science and business. Still, something was missing. Tesla needed a way to broadcast his name on a grand scale.

8 MEETING OF THE MINDS

Y ou could argue that without legendary producer Berry Gordy, pop star Michael Jackson would never have become the "King of Pop." Gordy saw genius in young Michael, and it was through his guidance that Michael exploded onto the music scene. Further, those who witnessed the relationship between Howard Cosell and Muhammad Ali would agree that without Cosell the world would not have known Ali on the grand scale on which he dominated the American media. True, Ali, who was born as Cassius Clay, would have had a boxing career without Cosell's presence, but it was by way of the reporter's continual coverage that everyone came to love and respect the boxer who floated like a butterfly and stung like a bee. Likewise, in the scientific world it can be said that without Thomas Commerford Martin, there wouldn't have been a Nikola Tesla, and perhaps no alternating current. For without the man known as "T.C." to most, it's doubtful Nikola Tesla would have grown in reputation and notoriety as he did.

T. C. Martin—a man of distinguished physical features: a shaved head, piercing eyes, and a gaudy mustache—was a professional writer who had worked for Thomas Edison from

1877 to 1879. In search of a change in scenery, he left on good terms with Edison and settled in Jamaica for a short time before returning to New York in 1883 as editor of the moderately successful scientific journal *Operator and Electric World*. Using his relationship with Edison, T.C. brought the publication into the spotlight by featuring the father of invention on a regular basis. Before long, T.C.'s name became known and well respected in scientific circles—seen as an affable visionary with a natural intuition for marketing and social promotion—but he wanted more out of his job, leading him to organize an internal coup at *Operator and Electric World*. With coeditor Joseph Wetzler by his side, they left for *Electrical Engineer*, which soon became the most respected publication in the field due to T.C.'s reputation and the quality of work he helped produce. In 1887, T.C. was named president of the newly formed American Institute of Electrical Engineers (AIEE), an organization that would advance his career, and later Nikola Tesla's.

Model of Tesla's AC induction motor

In July 1887, T.C. learned about Tesla and his alternating current experiments. Intrigued, he set up a visit to his Liberty Street laboratory.

Immediately impressed by Tesla's brilliant ideas and his confident demeanor, T.C. talked Tesla into being featured in the publication. T.C. commented that Tesla had "eyes that recall all the stories one has read of keenness of vision and phenomenal ability to see through things. He is an omnivorous reader, who never forgets . . . A more congenial companion cannot be desired."

An important relationship had been formed, one that would last for decades and result in mutual gains on both sides and also produce the most important compilation of Tesla's writings in 1893, edited by T.C., aptly titled *The Inventions, Researches and Writings of Nikola Tesla.*

In 1888, though, the problem was that Tesla's name was not known like Edison's, and Tesla didn't have the desire to self-promote nor the skills to do so. This was, remember, the boy who had once tried to compliment one aunt by explaining that she was not as ugly as the other. In Tesla's own mind, he was an immigrant who still had much to learn about the American way of life. He needed to find a way to get his name out there, and T. C. Martin was the perfect man to help him do this.

At the beginning of the year, T.C. arranged for former Cornell University engineering professor and esteemed scientist William Anthony to test Tesla's AC motors for efficiency. T.C. realized Tesla needed a respected person in the field to vouch for his work, and he believed Anthony, who had recently accepted a new position at Mather Electric Company in Connecticut, was the person they needed to stand behind Tesla's AC invention.

William Anthony

With his unkempt beard catching the eye of all who met him, misleading some to believe he was more of a lumberjack than an academic, Anthony came to the Liberty Street lab upon T.C.'s request. Anthony's tests continually yielded great results. In turn, Tesla agreed to visit Cornell to display his motors to professors and students. After thorough tests had concluded, Anthony was certain Tesla had something special with his alternating current system. T.C. and Anthony urged Tesla to present at an upcoming AIEE convention, one that would hold attendance of some of the most brilliant—and most important—scientific minds in the world.

Tesla shuddered at the idea of presenting in front of a large group of experts. It wasn't a lack of knowledge that worried him; it was the large audience that bothered him. If Tesla had had his wish, he would have been perfectly content hiding himself in his laboratory away from as many people as possible.

Adding to Tesla's unwillingness to give the lecture was the fact that although he had gotten over most of his apprehension that had resulted from the betrayal of Edison, Vail, and Lane, he still harbored some paranoia when it came to sharing his work publicly. As T.C. explained, Tesla was unwilling "to give the Institute any paper at all" on his work, so much so that he was not convinced by T.C. and Anthony to give the lecture until the day before the convention. Hastily, Tesla relented and wrote out everything in pencil on the eve of the presentation.

■ ■ ■ ■

May 15, 1888
American Institute of Electrical Engineers Convention,
Columbia College, New York, New York

"I now have the pleasure of bringing to your notice a novel system of electric distribution and transmission of power by means of alternate currents," said Tesla, with his eyes fixed on his audience. He had just started his lecture, which he had titled "A New System of Alternate Current Motors and Transformers," and he was poised and confident. His opening statements concluded with the assertion that his system would "establish the superior adaptability of these currents to the transmission of power."

T. C. Martin was impressed with Tesla's newfound authoritative presence, and he knew it was especially difficult because the majority of the electricians and engineers in attendance were opposed to alternating current. At the time of the lecture, Thomas Edison had already launched his campaign to promote DC and at the same time publicly scorn the effectiveness and safety of AC. There had been a few champions of AC—including the forerunner in the AC market, George Westinghouse—and the War of the Currents had already begun. The players in the war, though, had yet to fully surface.

Now here came Tesla Electric Company, which held the fundamental patents for Tesla's functional system, and people were watching with a skeptical eye. After all, only weeks earlier Thomas Edison had commented about George Westinghouse, saying, "Just as certain as death Westinghouse will kill a customer within six months after he puts in a system of any size . . . It will never be free from danger."

With the odds stacked against him, Tesla used diagrams, mathematical calculations, and carefully selected words to describe the oft-publicized problems with AC, which he followed with detailed, clearly stated solutions. As he presented his visuals and calculations, the engineers in attendance nodded in agreement, in shock that they had not thought of the very concepts Tesla was sharing with them. With his audience captivated, Tesla transitioned to a demonstration that showed how synchronous motors could be reversed in an instant. "A characteristic feature of motors of this kind is their capacity of being very rapidly reversed."

He also detailed his data on single-, two-, and three-phrase motors and even explained how they could easily be adapted with a DC apparatus. Never before had anyone displayed the manner in which AC could be used with DC machinery.

T. C. Martin looked on with pride. The sight of Tesla owning the stage was like seeing a masterful work of art that had once been a blank canvas. Without T.C.'s skilled use of his palette, this exhibition would not have been possible. Tesla continued while the attendees murmured excitedly—fully engaged.

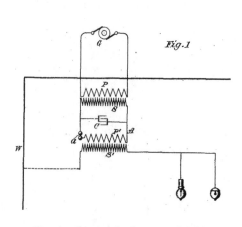

Drawing showing the function of Tesla's
high-frequency single-wire lighting

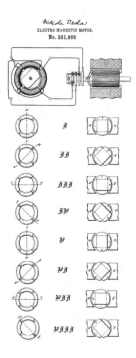

Tesla's AC induction motor patent sketch

After Tesla completed his lecture, William Anthony added support by claiming that his independent tests had shown Tesla's polyphase motors worked at slightly more than 60 percent efficiency. Anthony also noted that the direction of the current could be reversed "so quickly that it was almost impossible to tell when change took place." This ability to reverse the current swiftly was the key to sustained electric service without interruption and allowed AC to maintain the strength and output of the electricity. This was a complete contrast to DC, where the current fed in one direction from one circuit to the next, weakening the output the farther away from the power source you got.

By the conclusion of the lecture, Tesla had detailed his entire system with perfect clarity, spoken with authority, commanded the respect of the audience, and had an esteemed expert validate his claims. Nikola Tesla had had himself a *very* good day and confirmed his professional status.

■ ■ ■ ■

Tesla's fame soared immediately following the lecture. Among the most interested and enthusiastic attendees was a group of engineers who worked for George Westinghouse. Their boss had already been entertaining the idea of purchasing Tesla's patents, but when his engineers came back from the AIEE conference in awe of what they'd just witnessed, Westinghouse began negotiations in earnest with Brown and Peck.

Only six days after the lecture, Westinghouse sent his vice president Henry Byllesby to the Liberty Street lab, along with his lawyer Mr. Kerr. Although Byllesby admitted the science was beyond his intellectual grasp, he concluded that Tesla was a "straight-forward, enthusiastic" man. Fully impressed but at the same time conscious of business tactics, Byllesby and Kerr kept the meeting short to feign disinterest. As Byllesby and Kerr shook hands with Brown and Peck, the two Tesla Electric Company partners explained that they needed a decision by that Friday because there was an eager businessman in San Francisco they were negotiating with.

Westinghouse trusted Byllesby and Kerr, but he did not fall for the bluff of the mysterious San Francisco contact. Instead, he spent the next six weeks checking the validity of Tesla's work, sending different Westinghouse Electric representatives to test Tesla's machinery. Finally, at the constant urging of Thomas Kerr, Westinghouse concluded, "If the Tesla patents are broad enough to control the alternating motor business, then Westinghouse Electric Company cannot afford to have others own the patents."

The terms of the sale vary from source to source, with some claiming Westinghouse paid an even one million dollars for the patents, some claiming he paid one hundred thousand, while still others claiming he spent just over two hundred thousand. Regardless, all experts agree that Westinghouse spent a substantial sum of money for the outright possession of the forty patents, and it is unanimously confirmed that Tesla was supposed to receive royalties of $2.50 per watt produced from his motors.

And yet, even with the business matter settled and Tesla's

patents in the hands of Westinghouse, these two great men had not even met in person. To rectify that, Tesla was invited to Westinghouse's Pittsburgh laboratory, where he agreed to stay for an indefinite amount of time to help develop and effectively launch the AC system.

Tesla was in the middle of the happiest and most gratifying period of his life. The visions he'd seen in his mind throughout his childhood were now coming to life before his eyes. Nikola Tesla was a proud parent, alternating current his treasured child.

Nikola Tesla

George Westinghouse

Even better, Tesla was highly impressed with his new partner. In fact, he was in awe of the imposing George Westinghouse, taken by the six-foot-tall man with a thick swathe of hair and equally full sideburns that led down to his signature walrus handlebar mustache. Upon their initial meeting, Tesla admitted that his "first impression [was of a man with] tremendous potential of energy . . . A powerful frame, well proportioned, with every joint in working order, an eye as clear as crystal, a quick springy step—he presented a rare example of health and strength. Like a lion in a forest, he breathed deep and with delight the smoky air of his factories."

This high opinion was not limited to Nikola Tesla, as

Westinghouse had gained a flattering reputation over the course of his adult life. But nothing Westinghouse had gained—reputation included—had been simply handed over to him. Instead, Westinghouse was a true self-made man who had earned respect and trust and with it, great success.

9 EARNED SUCCESS

With Westinghouse not only in the fold but now leading the charge to introduce alternating current to the world on a grand commercial scale, Edison and his financiers, namely J. P. Morgan, realized they had an imminent threat at hand. After all, George Westinghouse was loved and respected by many and viewed—like Edison—as a self-made man.

From the day he came into the world in Central Bridge, New York, on October 6, 1846, George Westinghouse Jr. was prone to fits of frustration and stubbornness. While his tantrums as an infant included crying hysterically, they turned into more physical displays as he grew older, becoming so severe that he would beat his head against the wall until he got his way.

"I had a fixed notion that what I wanted I must have," George would later conclude. "Somehow, that idea has not entirely deserted me throughout my life. I have always known what I wanted, and how to get it. As a child, I got it by tantrums; in mature years, by hard work."

As a boy, his fits would earn him a reputation around town and in school, and he was soon fighting any of the many boys who called him crazy, even those bigger than him. After one such fight, George Sr. took his son to the barn to beat him with a switch as consequence for the altercation, and upon the weak switch breaking in half (George Jr. was big for his age), the young boy recommended to his father that he instead should use a leather harness that was hanging nearby, claiming it was stronger and wouldn't break. The beating ended, but George Jr.'s problem-solving and intuitive sense of invention had begun.

George Jr. showed little interest in school but was intrigued by all things mechanical. His father owned a machine shop, and soon—at the urging of an inspirational clergyman who believed his mechanical inclinations should be embraced, not shunned—George, at only thirteen years old, was given a full-time apprenticeship in the shop. The boss's son, George learned, needed to work even harder to earn respect, so he exerted all his energy in the shop to gain the respect of his senior colleagues.

One day, as the temperature soared near one hundred degrees, George Sr. had decided to give his employees the Saturday afternoon off. However, an order came in soon after that required a number of pipes to be cut to a specific size. Young George, being the lowest-ranking employee, was given the job and told to stay and work until it was finished. George fumed at first, promising to himself that if he ever ran his own business, he would give all his employees every Saturday afternoon, and even Sundays, off—a practice he started later in life, which not only began a Westinghouse business custom of having weekends off, but contributed to it becoming a national custom as well.

As George began dragging pipes to the sawhorse—still mad

about the extra work his father had assigned him—he eyed the steam engine and the lathe.

An idea struck him.

George mounted the pipes to the lathe and used steam power and the saw to slice through the pipes like butter. Although it would have taken him the rest of the day to cut the pipes with the saw by hand, with the steam-powered lathe the job was done in less than an hour. He returned home to a furious George Sr., who did not believe his son's claim that the job was done. But after he returned to the shop with young George and saw the pipes were all perfectly sized, the two walked home with the elder's arm firmly around the smiling youngster. An inventor had been born.

In the years that followed, George toyed with minor inventions—including a rotary engine that would garner his first official patent—until everything came together with two of the most important inventions in his young career: the car replacer and the air brake.

The idea of the car replacer came to twenty-year-old George when he was en route from one of many trips from Central Bridge, New York, to other locations in New York to secure contracts for his father's company. As he was returning from a trip to Albany, he was delayed by a train accident ahead of his location.

George inquired about the delay, and a friend explained that two or three rear cars had jumped the tracks and needed to be placed back on the rails. After witnessing the long and monotonous task of getting the cars back on the tracks, George commented that "they could have done the whole thing in fifteen minutes by clamping a pair of rails to the track, and running them off at an angle like a frog [a device used to allow trains to switch across tracks easily], so as to come up even against the wheels of the nearest derailed car. Then, by hitching an engine to the car, they could have shunted it back into place."

George immediately drew up plans and created a model, which he showed to his father. George Sr. was not impressed enough to offer financial backing, so George was forced to seek investors outside his family. The salesman in George came out, and he soon formed a partnership with two financiers. More important, this invention and experience brought him into close dealings with the railway, leading to the invention that would establish him as an influential person in the business world: the air brake.

Similar to the car replacer concept, the idea for the air brake came about on a trip, this one from Schenectady to Troy. Again, a rail accident delayed George's trip, an accident that was more severe than the previous one and had resulted in two freight trains crashing into each other and creating a massive mess in their wake.

This accident, thankfully, hadn't brought about any casualties, but George knew that had the cars been passenger locomotives, the cost would have been deadly.

As was his nature, George asked railway officials why this accident had occurred. The weather was clear and there were no signs of obstruction or faulty tracks. He learned that it had been due to the fact that you "can't stop a train in a moment" because the method of stopping a train was hand-braking, which consisted of different brakemen applying brakes in each car, leading to uneven brake distribution. George quickly decided the problem was the gap of time between the engineer sounding the stop whistle and each brakeman applying the brakes on the wheels.

If the engineer could be the one to apply *all* the actual brakes and not just ring the alarm, a uniform braking system could be created that would be much safer.

George experimented with ways to apply brakes simultaneously and settled on the idea of a long chain that would run under the train and be secured in one burst, quickly hitching the brakes on each wheel at the same time. The remaining problem was how to distribute the power from the front to the back of the train.

One day while he was sitting at his desk, a woman approached George with a magazine, asking him to purchase a subscription to help her pay for training to be a teacher. George quickly said no and told the woman to try others who actually read magazines, but the woman said she had. George looked at the woman's face and was captured by a charitable feeling. He opened the magazine to a random spot, and that's when he saw an image that would lead to a successful air brake invention.

This image involved the Mont Cenis Tunnel—known today as the Fréjus Rail Tunnel—which runs through an elaborate mountain chain in the European Alps. It wasn't the image itself that captured Westinghouse's attention; it was how the tunnels were created. As he thumbed through the magazine, George learned that Italian engineers used compressed air as a motor to propel a locomotive up a steep mountain and had later decided that compressed air in conjunction with a drilling machine would allow them to bore their tunnel through the mountains. "The result has been a perforating machine," George read in awe, an epiphany forming in his mind, "moved by common air compressed to one sixth its natural bulk, and consequently, when set free, exercising an expansive force equal to six atmospheres."

Mont Cenis Tunnel entrance

Westinghouse decided that if compressed air could force pipe through the solid stone of a mountain, it could certainly power the length of a train to set brakes from the front to the back in an instant. He'd found the answer he'd been looking for in a magazine, of all things.

Complicated problems, like that of a braking system for trains, engrossed George and forced him to examine every angle. He worked out the kinks of the air brake and developed a functional system that would be much safer than the hand brakes.

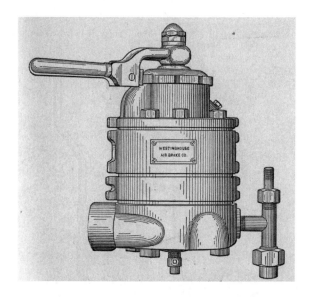

Westinghouse air brake

Through his natural sense of careful inspection and deduction, George developed his air brake system. Trials were run and improvements were made. George was ready to sell it and get his air brakes in steady use. Not only did he expect to make a profit, he also expected to make the railway safer. However, getting the brakes put to use wasn't easy. After waiting and waiting to meet the legendary "Commodore" Cornelius Vanderbilt, George was brushed off like lint, Vanderbilt laughing at the idea that "wind" could stop a train. Westinghouse struggled to find backing, but when he did and the air brake succeeded in trial runs for investors, Vanderbilt resurfaced and launched a campaign to smear George Westinghouse and the air brake in the public eye.

Vanderbilt ironically appealed to the demographic Westinghouse most often endeared himself to in his later business dealings: the workingman. With air brakes, there was a need for only one operator to apply the entire system, as the brakes worked simultaneously in all cars. With rail brakes, there was the necessity for multiple operators to apply them in each car (many operators meant many jobs, which meant many employed men). Vanderbilt went directly to the workforce, showing them that this silly "wind-powered" system would eliminate their jobs. Westinghouse, Vanderbilt claimed, didn't care about people: either in terms of the safety of the common man (as he claimed air brakes were flawed and dangerous) or in terms of valuing the workingman.

Westinghouse offered rebuttals, explaining that jobs would be created by his system, but Vanderbilt was too loud to silence, and he continued to portray Westinghouse in a negative light. To Westinghouse, ethics were as important as the inventions themselves, and Vanderbilt's unethical actions led George to vow *never* to stoop so low in his career.

In the end, a major tragic derailment of Vanderbilt's prized train, the Pacific Express, opened the door for Westinghouse—still only twenty-two years old—and he came into prominence and great financial success after he was issued his first air brake patent on April 13, 1869.

But George did not rest with the fully functional brake he had, and instead he perfected it and made it safer—*better*. The Pittsburgh-located Westinghouse Air Brake Company was established soon after, where George and his team would continually modify and perfect the system until it was an automatic air brake, which was patented in 1872. In the following years, Westinghouse made adjustments to his invention, steadily improving his product. Business boomed as more trains employed the air brake, which made it safer to travel on the rails.

It took just under a decade, but by the fall of 1881, Westinghouse's air brakes had been installed and utilized in the majority of the locomotives in the world. Westinghouse, now only thirty-five years old, had earned respect for his work ethic and attention to detail and also earned a reputation as a good employer, having regular dinners for his workers, giving away turkeys at Thanksgiving, and issuing bonuses. He kept to his word and gave weekends off, and he also introduced "piece work," the concept of being paid based on the work you do, not on a set pay, allowing his employees to earn more through increased production.

For George Westinghouse, much of what he invented came about because of reading. Just as he had come up with the idea for the air brake while reading a magazine, he would have an electric epiphany after reading a story in *Engineering* about an alternating current system on display in London. Like one of Tesla's flashes of light, a vision came to Westinghouse. He knew that this secondary generator mentioned in the article—that would come to be called a transformer—was the key to powering electric devices at different voltages over a wide span of territory.

Westinghouse also knew that at that very moment one of his employees, named Guido Pantaleoni, was in Italy due to the death of his father. He wired Pantaleoni to track down the inventors of this secondary generator, and in no time Pantaleoni found the two men responsible, Lucien Gaulard and John Gibbs. Though initial reports from Pantaleoni weren't flattering, Westinghouse soon bought an option on the American patent and arranged for one of the transformers to be delivered, along with a generator that was meant to run arc lighting on alternating current.

November 1885 brought Gaulard-Gibbs employee Reginald Belfield to Pittsburgh with a crate containing a Gaulard-Gibbs AC transformer. It was in such horrible condition, though, that Guido Pantaleoni initially wanted to send it back to Italy along with his complaints. Westinghouse had another idea. Instead of having a new, unknown transformer in tip-top shape, they had a transformer in need of a rebuild, and in that, they had the opportunity to learn about the machinery inside and out. Along with Belfield, Westinghouse disassembled and essentially built a whole new design that featured H-shaped iron plates as its core. This decision—keeping the shoddy transformer and re-designing it—turned it into the modern-day transformer. He had created a machine that could receive high voltages that spanned wide distances and could reduce the power for safe use in all buildings and homes.

On January 8, 1886, George Westinghouse officially entered the electricity business by incorporating Westinghouse Electric Company. From the formation of his company, he was met with internal grumblings that AC was not the answer, and instead was a waste of time. A dangerous one.

Westinghouse stayed the course with alternating current, believing strongly that this system would revolutionize the field. To begin, he decided to do the exact opposite of the showman Thomas Edison. Instead of announcing to the world that he had an amazing system that would change the way the world was run, Westinghouse kept his initial experiments a secret. There was no pomp and circumstance as there had been with all things Edison.

For Westinghouse, the idea was to have his leading electrician, William Stanley, who knew the workings of AC and the transformer as well as anyone, introduce the system to his hometown of Great Barrington, Massachusetts, where Stanley had built his own laboratory. With little press and no overt announcement or public ballyhoo that Stanley was using a novel alternating current system, the experiment took off, and more and more customers were added daily. Townsfolk were quickly won over in a month's time, and although the system had its kinks, the transformers were a success, indicating the time was right to officially launch Westinghouse Electric.

Westinghouse knew he needed to kick things off with a showplace, like Edison's brownstone in Manhattan. The four-story all-trade store of Adam, Meldrum & Anderson in downtown Buffalo served as the perfect setting for Westinghouse and his new system. Buffalo was quickly becoming a booming town of innovation and commercial activity, and the new all-purpose store had garnered a lot of chatter and anticipation as it was set to open. What better way to launch the system than by linking it to the launch of a much-talked-about business?

On November 27, 1886, the *Buffalo Commercial Advertiser* announced that Adam, Meldrum & Anderson was showcasing many useful items, along with 498 Stanley lights run by the Westinghouse system. "We were the first business house in the city to adopt the plan of lighting our stores by incandescence," the ad read. "Come and see the grandest invention of the nineteenth century."

Back in New York, Thomas Edison was fuming. While his public statement to reporters was for them to "tell [Westinghouse] to stick to air brakes," Edison knew this was the beginning of a competition that would require his complete energy and attention. George Westinghouse was lightning, and Edison knew thunder was soon to follow.

After all, this was George Westinghouse—the same person who, as a boy, would beat his head against the wall until he got his way—and Edison and his DC backers knew: this man would not simply go away. Not unless he was *forced* to.

10 THE RABID ANIMAL VERSUS THE FAWN IN THE FOREST

The entry of George Westinghouse into the field of electricity triggered a series of problems for Thomas Edison, resulting in one of the most trying years of Edison's professional life.

The year 1887 began with Westinghouse's alternating current system sinking its teeth into Edison's electric pie, taking an immediate bite out of future prospects and profits. Despite Edison's strong prediction that "just as certain as death Westinghouse will kill a customer within six months after he puts in a system of any size," from the get-go Westinghouse rounded up customers and implemented his system, free of casualties. In fact, by the end of the year, Westinghouse Electric Company had 68 central stations under contract. Even worse, Thomson-Houston Electric— known for arc lighting and already a chief competitor of Edison's— had partnered with Westinghouse, installing 22 Westinghouse transformers in 1887 alone. All told, after eight years in operation Edison Electric Company had 121 central stations, compared to close to 100 for Westinghouse in 1887 alone.

In *one* calendar year.

The numbers by themselves told Edison that George Westinghouse was a serious business threat.

One of the main issues, and a major contributing factor in Westinghouse's swift movement and success, was the fact that Edison's direct current system required multiple power stations as opposed to alternating current, which required only a single station on the outskirts of town. As Edison's trusted friend and publicist Edward Johnson attempted to explain, "We will do no small town business, or even much headway in cities of minor size." The system simply wasn't set up to accommodate small-town America. Edison turned his deaf ear to Johnson's warnings.

Thomas Edison continued to hear rumblings internally, along with some of his longer-tenured colleagues telling him he should switch systems immediately. Francis Upton, a Menlo Park veteran and trusted Edison employee, had firsthand knowledge and experience with the Hungarian ZBD alternating current system—named after inventors Károly Zipernowsky, Ottó Bláthy, and Miksa Déri—and made vehement pleas with his boss to buy an option and utilize the American rights. Edison bought the rights but refused to even consider using them. His purchase was more a ploy to keep possible competitors from using the ZBD system.

Instead, in October 1887, Edison and the brass of Edison Electric Light held firm publicly that producing and selling AC was an unwise business decision. As stated in the company's annual report of 1887, AC had "no merit in itself" commercially, and in terms of its safety, the high pressure of AC made it "notoriously destructive of both life and property." It was the company's opinion that it was only a matter of time before alternating current destroyed itself due to its volatile nature. All Edison Electric needed to do was withstand the initial surge and wait for the flames to rise. Edison himself reported to his board of executives that "[Westinghouse] cannot compete with us or do us any permanent harm, and that a steady conservative policy will win the battle."

Alternating current wasn't the only problem that charged toward Edison in 1887. Copper prices also threatened to stomp holes in the very foundation of Edison's direct current system, as a monopoly over copper goods had been attained by European businessman Hyacinth Secretan. With a firm grasp on the market, Secretan sent the ten-cent-per-pound price tag all the way up to seventeen cents per pound by late 1887.

Here again Edison owed blame to his direct current system's limitations and flaws. With the necessity of multiple power stations and multiple wires per stream of current, copper wire was essential. In contrast, alternating current needed a third of the amount of wire that direct current required. Just when Edison was already being squeezed out of profit due to the early success of Westinghouse's alternating current, now what profit remained was being sapped because of the system's reliance on copper wire. Edison was at the mercy of this European copper king, a man who seemed unconcerned with anything other than making an extra buck.

In November 1887, when Alfred P. Southwick wrote a letter to Edison asking him to vouch for the use of electricity as a more humane method of execution than the barbaric hangman's noose, Edison swiftly declined to get involved, making it clear that he was not in favor of capital punishment. But Thomas Edison, who once said, "No competition means no invention," knew he was involved in a battle. He just needed to find his chance to turn the tide back in his favor. Perhaps this Southwick fellow was offering to create the ripple needed to bring the current back in his favor.

In December 1887, Edison did a one-eighty and wrote to Southwick that the best, most humane manner of execution could be "accomplished by the use of electricity, and the most suitable apparatus for the purpose is that class of dynamo-electric machine which employs intermittent currents. The most effective of those are known as 'alternating machines.'" In his letter, Edison mentioned that the most prominent manufacturer of these machines was George Westinghouse, directly linking—he hoped—his main competitor with the death penalty. "The passage of the current from these machines through the human body even by the slightest contacts," Edison maintained, "produces instantaneous death."

With that, the year changed and so did the tide. Edison's official endorsement of AC as a mode of public execution put him back in control, and he was certain that 1888 would be nothing like 1887.

■　■　■　■

With Dr. Alfred P. Southwick now serving as the driving force behind alternating current being used as the next method of execution, Edison decided to take a bold public stance against Westinghouse and his system. After all, Edison knew it would take some time for the legal channels to be navigated by Southwick and his team. He'd wait to be called on by Southwick when the moment came, but he knew there was an opportunity here to take advantage of.

In the form of eighty-four bound pages, with a bloodred cover surrounding the bold title *A WARNING FROM THE EDISON ELECTRIC LIGHT COMPANY*, Edison Electric let everyone know in no uncertain terms that the alternating current system was equal to an electric plague on humanity. With contributions written by prominent members of the company, the book was composed by company president Edward Johnson and distributed to reporters and executives of various lighting utilities companies who were deciding which system to use.

Five "cautions" highlighted the contents of the long warning, ranging from "caution 1" on patent infringement on his light bulb to "caution 4" on the known and unknown dangers of alternating current. Of course, while Edison Electric maintained that such a deadly system needed to be kept from the general public, Edison himself was supporting AC to be used for the express purpose of killing when it came to capital punishment.

Thomas Edison, the most respected name in the scientific field of electricity, was directly warning the common man of the lurking dangers associated with alternating current, namely the system employed by George Westinghouse. "It is a matter of fact that any system employing high pressure, i.e. 500 to 2,000 units," it was explained in the red book, "jeopardizes life." In fact, a detailed listing of AC-induced fires suggested the high currents were just tempting fate to turn a building into an inferno. He then graphically chronicled the many fatal—and horrific—deaths as a result of AC that had been reported in newspapers around the country. At the same time, Edison made it clear that there was "no danger to life, health, or person, in the current generated by any of the Edison dynamos . . . and even the poles of the generator itself, may be grasped by the naked hand without the slightest effect." While alternating current was the rabid animal in the wild, direct current was the friendly fawn in the forest.

Pulling no punches, Edison was also urging "all electricians who believe in the future of electricity" to "unite in a war of extermination against cheapness in applied electricity." It was their responsibility to champion the proper use of electricity, which was direct current, and outlaw the detrimental system of Westinghouse. Edison had volunteered, as evidenced by his book, to lead the charge against alternating current.

■ ■ ■ ■

Meanwhile, the spring of 1888 brought not just the rebirth of nature's beauty but also the reentry of Nikola Tesla into the scientific field. The Serbian genius had filed a slew of patent applications related to alternating current, and people were talking. Tesla held public exhibitions and gained praise from the scientific press, but Edison wasn't concerned with this upstart scientist. Sure, he had been granted some forty patents in a short span of time. However, Edison had had intimate dealings with this man. Edison believed that although Tesla's mind was sharp, when it came to business tact, Tesla was severely outmatched.

That is, until Tesla teamed up with George Westinghouse in July 1888, threatening to land a few good punches and turn this into a knock-down, drag-out fight.

11 DEATH IN THE WIRES

March 12, 1888
New York, New York

Towers of white. Two stories high in some places, these towers had been erected overnight in downtown Manhattan. Mother Nature had been busy while most residents of New York City had been asleep, stacking snowflake atop snowflake to create the mounds of white—some that had crept dangerously close to the spiderwebbed wires overhead.

Only two days prior, the temperature had been a mild fifty degrees and city dwellers were tempted by talk of an early spring. But a ferocious arctic cold front had dipped south from Canada and mixed with a strong Gulf airstream from parts south. On March 11, when these two systems slammed into each other and wound together in a tight combination, temperatures plummeted quickly, accompanied by a pounding attack of rain. By the time the clock struck midnight on March 12, the temperature had dropped quickly, transforming the precipitation into freezing rain and sleet. Soon after, the winds kicked up to near sixty miles per hour, turning the sleet into heavy sideways snow.

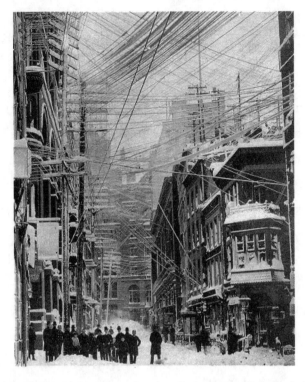

The Blizzard of 1888 led to the mandate that all wires in New York City be buried.

While most people slept through the worst of the storm— what would later be termed the "Great White Hurricane"—all forms of travel had shut down by sunrise, and the towering snow had trapped those who had been caught in the storm. These unlucky souls would either be rescued by good Samaritans with ladders or rope or fall victim to the elements, like the four hundred people on the East Coast who lost their lives as a result of the storm.

Yet another problem that had come with the storm was the impact of the rain and snow—and the severe winds—on the overhead wires. Places like Manhattan had lost communication with the outside world when telephone and telegraph wires sagged. Low temperatures combined with the overwhelming weight of the snow and the high winds and went on to break many lines altogether and scattered the remnants on the white surface not too far below. For the next few days, all modes of mass transportation were suspended, later resulting in the idea and discussion that perhaps there was a need for a manner of underground travel. Less than a decade later, subways found their way into major cities.

Major publications like the *New York Times* took the baton from the great storm and brought forth a tempest of reports and editorials attacking the manner in which high-voltage wires had been carelessly spread above almost every square inch of the city. "The city is liable to be put into darkness and the consequent perils," concluded the *Times*, urging—like many other papers— that all high-voltage wires be buried. The *Times* and a plethora of other periodicals focused on the inconveniences of electric wires, but this wasn't altogether unusual, since the electric wires and the nuisance that came with them had been a major topic of discussion since late in 1887, when the Edison Electric Company's many red books had been sprinkled around by one Thomas Alva Edison. Free of charge, of course.

This new wave of negative press for AC systems didn't help George Westinghouse's cause. Unfortunately for Westinghouse, it was only the beginning.

■　■　■　■

Moses Streiffer skipped his way down East Broadway toward Catherine Street, fully enjoying the nice weather that had taken over from the tragic storm a month prior. The boy was a peddler, selling buttons and combs and other small trinkets from a nearby stand.

The fifteen-year-old Romanian immigrant noticed a dangling telegraph wire by his side. As the boy approached the broken wire hanging down from the cedar post high above, he grabbed it. The sun was going down and the arc lights were showering their artificial rays toward the street, mixing in with the faint rays of sunshine soon to retire for the night.

Witnesses later said Moses had immediately continued skipping around and around the pole with wire in hand, as if he was involved in an entertaining game. The game was cut short, as was the boy's life, when a burst of sparks engulfed his body. After a flash of light, he fell to the ground and lay limp. Moses was dead.

Newspapers acknowledged the death of the Streiffer boy with articles and editorials, continuing their pleas to have the dangerous wires removed from overhead. In the end, the US Illuminating Company was charged with neglect for its loose wire, which had ended the boy's life.

■　■　■　■

May 11, 1888
616–618 Broadway, New York, New York

It had been a long day for workers from Brush Electric Company. They had spent much of their time cutting away dead wires from buildings high above the traffic on West Houston Street. A team of linemen were currently tackling the tough task of clearing a second-story cornice of dead wires. Among the workers was Thomas H. Murray, who was dangling from the cornice.

"I saw smoke curling in the window and heard a sputtering sound," an employee inside the building commented later on. Soon after spotting the wisp of smoke, workers found Murray dead beside an electric wire that was partially cut, the insulating material actively burning at the severed spot. Murray had failed to wear the required rubber gloves and had paid for the lapse in judgment with his life.

When others attempted to grab him and pull him from the cornice, they too were shocked by the live current. It took multiple sheets of rubber wrapped around Murray before the man's charred body could be helped off the cornice.

Newspapers broadcast the tragic story, adding to the building worry of common citizens everywhere.

■　■　■　■

June 5, 1888
201 West Forty-Fourth Street, New York, New York

He had written the letter on May 24. It had taken some time, but now, almost two weeks later, Harold Pitney Brown—a little-known electrical engineer—held open a copy of the *New York Evening Post.* He looked down his substantial nose, over his swollen handlebar mustache, and smiled as his eyes moved swiftly left to right.

"The death of the poor boy Streiffer," the letter began, "who touched a straggling telegraph wire on East Broadway on April 15, and was instantly killed, is closely followed by the death of Mr. Witte in front of 200 Bowery and of William [Thomas] Murray at 616 Broadway on May 11, and any day may add new victims to the list." Brown nodded as he read. He lifted a hand and touched the part in his hair with his index finger. "If the pulsating current is 'dangerous,' then the 'alternating' current can be described by no adjective less forcible than *damnable.*"

Brown focused intently as he read the portion that dealt with weakly insulated wire. "Among electric lighting men it is appropriately called 'undertaker's wire,' and the frequent fatalities it causes justify the name."

His eyes skipped to the end, where he demanded alternating current over three hundred volts be outlawed to save human lives from the same fate as Moses Streiffer, Fred Witte (who died on April 28 after touching a United States Company lamp), and Thomas H. Murray (who Brown had referred to as "William"

Murray in his letter). Earlier in Brown's letter, he had stated that "if the death of these three men can effect the adoption and enforcement of regulations similar to the following, they will not have died in vain." Brown reviewed his list of recommended regulations, nodding as he read about a limit of fifty lights on the same circuit, the necessity of a waterproof covering for outdoor arc light circuits, and ending with "no alternating current with a higher electromotive force than three hundred volts shall be used."

Harold P. Brown closed his paper and grinned. His opinion had been validated by at least one publication, the *New York Evening Post*, which was owned by one Henry Villard, who would one day happen to find himself president of Edison Electric Light Company.

■ ■ ■ ■

Only a few days later, Harold P. Brown was invited to attend a New York City Board of Electrical Control meeting on June 8, where his letter would be read word-for-word into the record before the board and then captured in the meeting's minutes and passed along to a host of respected electric companies and electricians, with George Westinghouse included.

Near the same time Brown's letter was being read before the Board of Electrical Control, George Westinghouse was in the process of writing his own letter, dated June 7, 1888—a letter addressed to none other than Thomas Alva Edison. In this letter, Westinghouse offered to come together and talk like adults and perhaps reach an agreement and form a truce between them. "I have a lively recollection of the pains that you took to show me through your works at Menlo Park when I was in pursuit of a plant for my house, and before you were ready for business . . . it would be a pleasure to me if you should find it convenient to make me a visit here in Pittsburgh when I will be glad to reciprocate the attention shown me by you."

Five days later, Thomas Edison responded in kind, declining the Westinghouse invitation with a curt written message: "My laboratory consumes the whole of my time." The following weeks found Edison and company claiming far and wide to the press that George Westinghouse was lying about his alternating current results.

Left with no hope for peace, Westinghouse knew he had to respond, but he did so by sticking to the facts related to alternating current, shedding light on the success and safety he had thus far exhibited. At the next New York City Board of Electrical Control meeting on July 16, Westinghouse presented a letter to the board, explaining that he had—in conjunction with Thomson-Houston—established 127 central stations in two years' time, while his Pittsburgh plant was the "largest incandescent lighting station in the world." He made it clear that when it came to safety, the numbers spoke for themselves. Not one of his 127 stations had experienced a fire, while a number of the 125 direct current stations had reported fires, three of which had completely destroyed the DC central stations. In regards to Thomas Edison's smear campaign, Westinghouse announced that he was taken aback by the "method of attack which has been more unmanly, discreditable and untruthful than any competition which has ever come to my knowledge."

It was clear, by way of written letters and through actions, that there would be no truce. Both sides knew: this was war. And it was just getting started.

■ ■ ■ ■

Just as he had done with Alfred P. Southwick (who was at that very moment still in the process of getting the next method of execution turned over to alternating current), Thomas Edison seized the chance to have someone else spearhead his fight against George Westinghouse. Instead of having his own face and name in opposition to his rival, here fate had handed him Harold P. Brown, a man who was a born fighter and who had come right out and called alternating current "damnable." Edison realized he wouldn't even need to do the discrediting himself; Brown would do the dirty work for him.

Late June 1888 found Harold P. Brown being called on by electricians and board members to actually prove his claims, while early July of the same year found Brown in the new West Orange laboratory of Thomas Edison attempting to do just that. Brown would later say it was he who had contacted Edison— although many would claim it was the opposite—in hopes of borrowing some equipment to aid in his experiments. "To my surprise," said Brown, "Mr. Edison at once invited me to make experiments at his private laboratory, and placed all necessary apparatus at my disposal."

Harold P. Brown set up shop in Edison's fancy laboratory for much of July, where he even had the full cooperation and assistance of Edison employee Arthur Kennelly and Edison's most trusted colleague, Charles Batchelor.

By the end of July, Brown was confident that he had gathered enough evidence to prove alternating current was deadly beyond any semblance of a doubt. After issuing invitations to all Board of Electrical Control members, representatives from all electric light companies, prominent members of the electrical fraternity, and members of the press, Brown greeted just over seventy guests at Columbia College. He was intent to prove his case.

■ ■ ■ ■

July 30, 1888
Professor Chandler's Lecture Room,
Columbia College, New York, New York

Harold P. Brown stood upright before his esteemed audience. Each person watching him knew his name, and now everyone knew what he looked like. He raised his hand to his slicked hair and ran his open palm over his head.

"I represent no company and no commercial or financial interest," he said with a serious stare. That point made, Brown explained the fundamental differences between alternating and direct current, making eye contact with the many electricians in attendance, as if to say, "This part isn't for you, my friends. I only detail the differences for the layperson who is otherwise unaware."

Noticing some expressions of disinterest, Brown quickly

walked to the middle of the room and stood beside a large wooden cage with copper wires woven between the bars. "Over the last few weeks, I have proved by repeated experiments that a living creature could stand shocks from a continuous current much better." Brown lowered his hand to the cage beside him. People in the audience shifted in their seats, reporters looking at the electricians in the room, searching for answers, the electricians shrugging and scratching their heads.

Brown suddenly disappeared into another room. A moment later, he walked back into the room holding a leash connected to a large black retriever. Tugging on the leash, Brown led the dog to the cage and forced it inside. After strapping the dog inside, Brown slammed the barred door and locked it. Gasps and sighs could be heard from the audience; a nervous chattering wafted over the area as people wondered what this man was doing.

Brown did not keep them guessing. Instead, he announced that the dog—which weighed seventy-six pounds—was in good health and had no inclinations to hostility. Brown nodded to two men at the side of the room, Arthur Kennelly and Dr. Frederick Peterson, who scurried to the cage and held the dog in place while electrodes were attached to its right foreleg and left hind leg.

Brown called for three hundred volts and Arthur Kennelly flicked a switch and turned a dial and the dog shimmied left and right in the cage. The chattering in the audience grew silent. Eyes widened.

Brown gave the order for four hundred volts, then seven hundred.

The sound of scraping claws reverberated around the room, and the dog whined between bursts of movement. It broke free of the restraints, and Brown's team of "scientists" were forced to open the cage and reattach the straps. More and more people voiced their displeasure about the spectacle before them.

Brown demanded a thousand volts and all whining and yelping ceased and was replaced by a clenched snout that shook like a leaf in a hurricane. Some guests dashed from the room; others begged Brown to have mercy.

Harold P. Brown gestured for Kennelly to stop.

"Now," said Brown with a sly grin, "he will have less trouble when we try the alternating current." Kennelly and Peterson assisted Brown in hooking the dog and the cage up to a Siemens Brothers alternator.

Brown stepped a few feet away from the cage as Kennelly looked at him curiously. Brown called for three hundred volts and Kennelly set the current as commanded and turned it on. The dog shifted left and right briefly before collapsing inside the cage.

Dead.

As Brown smiled again, satisfied, he gave Kennelly the signal to turn off the current.

Agent Hankinson, a member of the ASPCA, stepped forward and forbade Brown from experimenting on any other animal.

One after another, audience members rushed from the lecture hall. While some voiced their disgust with the cruelty of the exhibition, others made a point of contention that it wasn't so much the alternating current that had done the dog in, but instead it was the extended torture with direct current that had considerably weakened the dog's state.

A smug Brown assured the dissenting audience that he had plenty of other dogs that he had experimented on in the past month, claiming the "treachery" of alternating current was to blame for the quick death of the dog. It was later discovered that Brown had enlisted local neighborhood boys to gather up stray dogs by applying a bounty of twenty-five cents per canine. Before saying farewell to his guests, Brown announced that the fatality threshold for the many dogs he'd experimented on had been three hundred volts for alternating current and over a thousand volts for direct current. Before his visitors left, they received Brown's final thoughts that the "only places where an alternating current ought to be used were the dog pound, the slaughter house, and the state prison."

■ ■ ■ ■

August 3, 1888
Professor Chandler's Lecture Room,
Columbia College, New York, New York

Harold P. Brown looked around at the audience, a more condensed group than he'd welcomed a few days ago, but then again, this time he had been more selective. This crowd contained most of his colleagues, a few experts in the field of electricity, a handful of public health officials, and a generous helping of reporters.

"All of the physicians present," Brown announced as he stood next to three cages that already housed captive dogs, "expressed the opinion that a dog had a higher vitality than a man, and that, therefore, a current which killed a dog would be fatal to a man."

Without further delay, Brown started the display with a sixty-one-pound dog in cage number one, which he disposed of in short order with three hundred volts of alternating current. There was no struggle. No whining. No yelping. No mess. Just a few seconds' time and a dead dog where a live one once sat.

Not to be outdone by dog number one, Brown moved on to the second cage, which held a ninety-one-pound Newfoundland. Only eight seconds were needed for an equally clean execution of this larger dog.

Pleased with the results thus far, Brown smiled as he moved on to the final cage. Inside was a fifty-three-pound mutt. But Brown's smile soon faded when the dog lasted a whopping four minutes—suffering, whining, and struggling—before keeling over for good.

With his second presentation complete, Harold P. Brown regained his smile and bid his guests a fond farewell.

■ ■ ■ ■

In the month following Brown's three-dog display, Thomas Edison met more good fortune when the New York state legislature, thanks to Alfred P. Southwick's guidance, officially designated electrocution as its new mode of capital punishment.

The state legislature created a new committee to secure

advice from people who were knowledgeable about the deadly impact of electricity. This committee appointed Dr. Frederick Peterson as its chairperson. Peterson was one of Edison's men, and the same man who had helped Brown with both his displays at Columbia College.

Teaming up once again, Brown and Peterson happily accepted the generous offer of Thomas Edison to use his West Orange laboratory to continue their "research" on how best to kill living creatures with electricity. Soon after, at a summative meeting on November 15, Dr. Peterson told the rest of the committee that both currents would kill but that alternating current was the preferable and recommended choice.

The committee announced that it would make its decision official on December 12 at its next meeting, but Harold P. Brown wasn't about to leave this matter with any uncertainty. Instead, he organized yet another electrical demonstration that would make it 100 percent clear that alternating current was the only option.

Brown knew what he needed: to show how larger animals reacted to alternating current.

■   ■   ■   ■

December 5, 1888
Edison Laboratory, West Orange, New Jersey

Harold P. Brown had pitched it as a "matter of great importance" to his esteemed audience, made up of several reporters, employees of Edison Electric, physicians from the Medico-Legal

Society, and two members of the newly formed Gerry Commission (the "Death Commission"), Alfred P. Southwick and Elbridge T. Gerry.

Among this well-respected and highly regarded group, one man stood out and brought great value to the group as a whole: Thomas Edison. Up to this point, Edison had only been a supplier of space and material for Brown's experiments. He'd remained silent as to Brown's research with animals. But now here he was in plain sight. With his mere presence he'd legitimized the entire spectacle. Reporters now looked to Brown with a newfound sense of respect, as did the members of the Gerry Commission and the Medico-Legal attendees.

Brown began his demonstration by revealing a calf, which took only thirty seconds to be done away with. Brown followed this by disposing of a larger calf and then did the same with a horse.

The next day, the *New York Times* declared that what had been witnessed in West Orange had proven that alternating current was the "most deadly force known to science, and that less than half the pressure used in this city for electric lighting [1,500–2,000 volts] by this system is sufficient to cause instant death." In this one statement, Thomas Edison had achieved what he'd hoped for, in that it was now on record that alternating current was the "death current." On the flip side, direct current now looked like a safe mode of delivering electricity to the public— far more safe and reliable than a system that was now synonymous with death.

A few days later, the Medico-Legal Society officially adopted "death by alternating current" and listed its recommendations for how to administer the current to criminals. Edison must have been doubly giddy to add "executioner's current" to alternating current's list of nicknames. Adding even more fuel to the fire, Edison would recommend that executing someone with electricity should be referred to as being "Westinghoused."

In response to Harold P. Brown's assertion that he'd proven without any doubt that three hundred volts of alternating current was deadly, George Westinghouse told numerous New York papers that "a large number of persons can be produced who have received a one-thousand-volt shock from alternating current without injury." He summed up his company's rebuttal by stating, "We have no hesitation in charging that the objects of these experiments is not in the interest of science or safety." While some in his camp wanted him to return the smear campaign with similar methods, Westinghouse refused to fight dirty. When asked why he didn't go after Edison by returning his vicious attack, Westinghouse explained he had learned that you "don't play the other fellow's game." When Ernest H. Heinrichs, a newspaper reporter Westinghouse hired to promote his company in a positive manner, implied that perhaps that was what was needed, Westinghouse firmly refused. "By letting the others do all the talking," Westinghouse told Heinrichs, "we shall make more friends in the end than if we lower ourselves to the level of our assailants."

Harold P. Brown, though, did not appreciate Westinghouse's

statement that he was not being truthful about the deadly nature of alternating current. In a surreal turn of events, Brown essentially challenged Westinghouse to a sort of electric duel straight out of an old Western movie: "I challenge Mr. Westinghouse to meet me in the presence of competent electrical experts and take through his body the alternating current while I take through mine a continuous [direct] current." In multiple publications, Brown explained his electric game of chicken in great detail, making it clear he was completely serious. "We will commence with 100 volts, and will gradually increase the pressure 50 volts at a time . . . until either one or the other has cried enough, and publicly admits his error."

Ever the professional, Westinghouse never responded to this odd offer to duke it out with electricity. He had no comment whenever it was brought up in public.

Westinghouse publicly opposed the idea of using electricity to kill criminals, but it had been accepted as the most humane method of execution. The wheels had been set in motion. In fact, a key member of the team charged with creating the electric killing machine—soon to be the electric *chair*—was none other than Harold P. Brown, named the electrical expert on the design team.

Now the only question was, who would be the first person to receive such a death sentence?

Enter William Kemmler.

12 SHOCKED...

Feet slapped the floor at a rhythmic pace, steadily growing louder. Frank Fish stood up and extended a hand. In the other, he held his banjo, worn around the edges and significantly yellowed. It might have been old and stained from constant use, but it had been a source of needed entertainment for Fish and his cellmate, William Kemmler. For the last couple of hours the two had been performing "My Old Kentucky Home" and other songs to pass the time.

Earlier that day, in late afternoon, Reverend Dr. Houghton and Chaplain Yates had come to read Kemmler his last rites, later commenting to the press that Kemmler had seemed anxious, regretful, and ready for the end. After the final blessings had been given, a thunderstorm—riddled with lightning strikes—flashed blinding light into Kemmler's cell. Even the man who'd said he was "ready to die" couldn't help but flinch as thunder boomed and lightning snapped.

Around the time Fish took out his banjo, the storm passed, giving way to a peaceful sunset.

The cadence of steps stopped abruptly. The iron latches clicked with an echo; prison guard Daniel McNaughton yanked open the cell door and gave Kemmler a short nod. Kemmler gripped Fish's hand and then nodded back at the guard. He knew McNaughton, his principal keeper, had been kind in letting the men stay up until this late hour. McNaughton had also shown humanity over the last few days by reading *Les Misérables* to Kemmler.

"Keep your courage up, Kemmler, it will all be over soon. I will follow you after a little while," said Fish, who was also condemned to death, though he'd be spared a year later when his sentence was changed to life in prison.

Kemmler shook Fish's hand. "I guess I will behave all right. It can't come too soon for me. Being so near the end is as bad as the actual going."

The two death row cellmates let go of each other's hands, Fish's banjo swinging by his side as he and McNaughton left Kemmler alone in his cell.

Any fleeting hopes Kemmler might have had of winning an appeal and escaping the deathly electric experiment had been dashed not long before, when lawyer Bourke Cockran had nobly fought to prove the electric chair would be just as, if not more, inhumane and cruel than the hangman's noose. After Thomas Edison had been placed in the witness stand in late July and testified that the electric chair was indeed more humane than the gallows and was therefore the proper method of execution, the appeal was shot down. There was no disputing the guarantee of the great Thomas Edison. To most, his words were as powerful and certain as God's. As the *Albany Journal* later explained, "The Kemmler case at last has an expert that knows something concerning electricity. Mr. Edison is probably the best informed man in America, if not the world, regarding electric currents and their destructive powers." Bourke Cockran had no choice but to concede the appeal, though his closing remarks warned that the decision was bound to bring tragedy the likes of which the world hadn't yet experienced.

Unable to sleep, William Kemmler signed his name onto scraps of paper—his autograph was now highly sought-after, and he wanted to repay the people who'd shown him kindness during the last few months, especially Gertrude Durston, the warden's wife, who had taught him how to sign his name. Having never learned to read or write, Kemmler had grown proud of this newfound skill. When every piece of paper had been signed, Kemmler lay down and closed his eyes.

■ ■ ■ ■

August 6, 1890, 5:50 a.m.
Auburn Prison, Upstate New York

"William, it's time," said Warden Charles Durston, his voice shaky.

William Kemmler sat on his cot in a gray sack coat and vest and yellow patterned pants. He wore a white shirt under the vest, with a black-and-white bow tie. He ran his hand over the freshly shaven patch atop his head and nodded at prison guard Joseph Velling, who folded the razor and placed it in his pocket.

Kemmler looked back at the warden and started to stand. "I'm ready to go."

The warden held up his hand, motioning for Kemmler to remain seated. The jittery warden reached into his breast pocket and produced an official document. With a sigh, he recited the new death warrant, hesitantly reading, "By a current of electricity sufficient to cause death."

Kemmler got to his feet and Velling cut a slit in the man's trousers at the base of the spine. This would be where one of the electrodes would be attached, while the other would be attached securely to the new bald spot on his scalp.

Warden Durston turned, passed through the open iron-barred door, and walked down the hall; Kemmler and Velling followed.

It was a short death march, as the chamber that housed the electric chair was only down the hall from Kemmler's basement cell. Oddly, the room was lit by gaslight, not electric bulbs. Twenty-seven witnesses—two of them handpicked reporters—sat in a wide, arching semicircle inside the death chamber as William Kemmler entered. One witness said the convicted murderer was a "spruce looking, broad-shouldered little man."

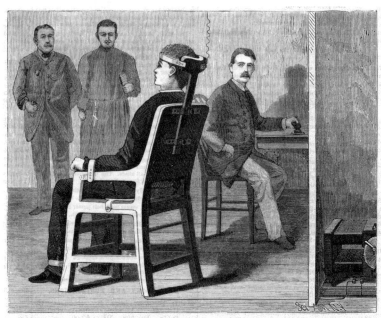

EXECUTION BY ELECTRICITY, SHORTLY TO BE INTRODUCED IN N. Y. STATE.

Sketch of Kemmler execution in *Scientific American*

Warden Durston led Kemmler to the square, high-backed chair located in the center of the back wall, the witnesses half-encircling him now. The wooden chair, which many said reminded them of an easy chair, had a seat of perforated wood and arms two inches wide, with three wooden braces across the back, the upper two fastened to a hard rubber cushion. A rounded rubber cup—the lower electrode inside—jutted inward from the bottom of the chairback, with a wire trailing toward the far wall. A metal cap hung stiffly from an adjustable arm at the top of the chair, a long wire leading up to the ceiling. Inside the cap was the upper electrode, which would be placed against

Kemmler's scalp. A small sponge surrounded each electrode to allow better contact and prevent scorching of the flesh.

"Give me a chair," announced Warden Durston, startling the witnesses, who thought he was referring to the chair of death. A regular kitchen chair was pushed forward, in front of and slightly to the right of the electric chair, and Kemmler was directed to sit down facing the witnesses. Warden Durston asked for another chair and placed it next to the seated Kemmler. He put his arm around Kemmler's shoulders.

"Now, gentlemen, this is William Kemmler," said Durston. Kemmler bowed slightly toward the audience. "I have just read the death warrant to him and have told him he has got to die," said Durston. The warden's hands and voice trembled. He turned toward Kemmler. "Have you anything to say?"

William Kemmler began to stand but instead remained seated. "Gentlemen, I wish you all good luck," he said, gazing over the crescent moon of onlookers. "I believe I am going to a good place, and I am ready to go. I want only to say that a great deal has been said about me that is untrue. I am bad enough. It is cruel to make me out worse." He bowed again and then rose to his feet.

The warden motioned to Kemmler. "Take off your coat," he ordered, his voice still unsure. He then cut off the tail of the shirt, which had been sticking through the slit in the man's trousers, exposing his bare skin for the lower electrode. "Sit there," he said, pointing to the electric chair.

Velling and Durston fastened the eleven straps to secure Kemmler's body to the chair. The warden's hands were shaking.

Kemmler whispered, "My God, Warden, can't you keep cool? Take your time."

The metal cap was lowered onto the shaved spot on Kemmler's head, the electrode inside pressed firmly to his scalp.

Dr. Fell emerged with a syringe. He applied a generous amount of saltwater solution to the sponges. When his job was done, he moved back and stood beside Alfred P. Southwick, who was staring at his invention, which was now, before his very eyes, fully realized.

The warden placed a leather mask over Kemmler's face. He tightened the straps so the nose was pressed back, Kemmler's mouth the only portion still visible to witnesses.

Dr. Edward Charles Spitzka, the principal doctor in charge, moved to the back of the chair and placed the lower electrode through the clothing and against the skin at Kemmler's spine. "God bless you, Kemmler."

Kemmler nodded slightly.

The multiple physicians present had debated how long the current should be left on. In the end, they decided Dr. Spitzka would give the command when the current should begin and when it should end. The plan was to hold the charge for twenty seconds. Dr. Spitzka asked for and received a stopwatch to keep the time.

Two doctors inspected the straps and connections to make

sure everything was set up according to plan. After they both conferred and agreed it was ready, one said, "God bless you, Kemmler, you have done well."

The witnesses, many of whom were shaking, sweating, and tearing up, now nodded in agreement. "You have," said a few of them.

Warden Durston moved over to the wall separating the death chamber from a small room. Inside this control room, Edwin F. Davis, a prison electrician, was in charge of a switchboard that held the many knobs and switches. Like spaghetti noodles, wires jutted out from the board and trailed through the window and up to the roof. The wires snaked around the prison's signature dome and then dropped down into a room on the second floor that held the massive dynamo, almost a thousand feet from the death chamber.

"Ready?" Warden Durston asked the control room. A knock on the wall signaled the dynamo had reached the proper voltage. Durston turned to the physicians. "Do the doctors say it is all right?"

Dr. Spitzka looked at his team, who nodded. Then he looked back at the masked Kemmler and said again, "God bless you."

Kemmler nodded as he had before.

Dr. Spitzka addressed the warden. "All right."

"Goodbye," Durston said softly to Kemmler, his voice still uneven. He rapped on the wall twice, which was the preset signal to the control room that it was time.

Edwin F. Davis watched the bulbs in the control room light up. The voltage was set. He pulled down the switch that placed the chair in circuit.

Back in the chamber, Kemmler's body stiffened. His fingers grasped the chair as his chest bulged forward against the restraints. The index finger of his right hand bent with such force it pressed his nail into his palm, blood dripping from the laceration. His mouth twitched and grimaced, but no sound came from his lips.

Witnesses wriggled in their seats like they felt the current, too, and many looked away from the dying man.

Dr. Spitzka held the stopwatch to his face, where he saw it had been ten seconds, and then peered back at Kemmler.

"Stop!" he cried a moment later. The command echoed throughout the room.

Warden Durston rapped hard on the wall again, prompting Davis to pull the switch to take the chair out of circuit. It had been seventeen seconds.

Instantly, Kemmler's body relaxed and slumped against the eleven straps holding him to the chair.

"He's dead," said Dr. Spitzka.

Spitzka asked the other doctors to examine the body to confirm death, pointing out the paleness of his skin, the brightened nose. The doctors nodded in agreement, and by all accounts, William Kemmler had been successfully executed by way of electricity, in a mere seventeen seconds.

Warden Durston detached the electrode from Kemmler's

head by lifting the metal cap a few inches. Witnesses that made up the scientific community immediately began to congratulate one another and shake hands, as many of them were there only to witness the manner in which the chair would work. All appeared pleased—this had been a successful experiment.

Alfred P. Southwick stepped forward and faced the satisfied witnesses. A decade in the making, and this was his moment. He gestured toward Kemmler's limp body. "There is the culmination of ten years' work and study." Southwick wore a wide grin. He knew this was a significant victory for his invention, and he also knew Thomas Edison had just experienced a crucial moment in his battle against alternating current. He cleared his throat and continued. "We live in a higher civilization from this day."

But Southwick's speech was cut short when a witness pointed to the blood dripping in pulsating fashion from the cut on Kemmler's hand, which had been caused by his fingertip digging into his palm.

Eyes grew wide; the doctors exchanged worried looks. If the blood was still dripping from the wound, it meant his heart had to be beating.

"Great God!" cried one of the doctors.

Kemmler's chest heaved. "See," said another doctor. "He breathes!"

"Turn on the current!" hollered Dr. Spitzka. "Turn on the current, instantly! This man is alive!"

13 ...TO DEATH

August 6, 1890, 6:45 a.m.

Auburn Prison, Upstate New York

The witnesses' faces grew as pale as Kemmler's skin.

Kemmler's body twitched slightly. The onlookers stepped back on instinct. Alfred P. Southwick, who moments before had begun a victory speech, moved back to the far wall and stood next to Dr. Fell. They watched.

Kemmler groaned.

One of the two reporters present called out, "For God's sake, kill him and have it over." Then the man fainted and was caught by neighboring witnesses. They laid him down on a nearby bench and fanned air on his face.

Blood trickled from Kemmler's ruptured hand to the floor, a small puddle forming quickly.

"Have the current turned on," Dr. Spitzka shouted to Durston.

The warden was a visible mess, shaking and trembling. He dashed to the wall and rapped twice, but nothing happened.

A thousand feet away, in the second-floor room, the massive dynamo had been powered down. Edwin F. Davis sent a two-bell alarm to the men in charge of the dynamo, the heart of the device, signaling them to turn the machine back on at once. But there was a problem. Since Dr. Spitzka and Durston had already ordered the dynamo shut down, the voltmeter was near zero. It needed time to kick back into gear and reach sufficient voltage. Davis couldn't open the circuit and run current to the chair until the dynamo had been powered up.

All anyone could do was wait. A minute passed.

Kemmler's groaning turned into a strained wheeze at regular intervals, as if he was desperately trying to breathe.

Two witnesses got sick; several were forced to turn away. The unconscious reporter was still being fanned as he lay on the bench.

George T. Quinby, the district attorney who had prosecuted Kemmler, was so unnerved he rushed from his chair and out of the chamber, holding his stomach. He later passed out in the hallway.

Two minutes after the command had been given to restart the current, the voltmeter held the proper reading and Davis signaled that the charge was coming.

Durston looked at the doctors, who all stepped away from Kemmler's body quickly, not wanting to have the current jump from him to them.

Durston knocked twice and a click came from the other side of the wall as Davis opened the circuit.

Kemmler's body shot into a statuesque pose, back arched and chest puffed out. The straps grew taut and creaked to restrain him. There was no more sound from Kemmler's mouth— no groaning or wheezing.

Dr. Spitzka cautiously moved closer to examine Kemmler's body, but Warden Durston made it clear how this round would go as he yelled to Edwin F. Davis in the control room, "Keep it on! Keep it on!"

Kemmler's head smoked. In haste, the electrode had not been securely fastened as before, and the sponge now held little saltwater solution. A spark formed in the space between the electrode and the bare spot on his scalp, scorching the skin and giving off a smell of burning flesh that hung like a cloud in the death chamber. The lower back of the chair seemed to catch fire, but it was actually the other electrode as it also sparked and set the back of the vest and shirt aflame.

Dark spots—a combination of purple and black—formed on the visible parts of Kemmler's skin.

Finally, Warden Durston called out, "Cut the current! Cut the current!"

Davis shut down the death machine for good.

How long the current had been left on would be a source of great debate in the days to come. Some claimed it was on for four and a half minutes, while others said two. The official report, though, stated William Kemmler had received two thousand volts of electricity for seventy seconds.

Someone extinguished the flames on Kemmler's back, leaving a smoking lump of mutilated body. Many witnesses got sick again. The team of doctors examined Kemmler thoroughly, taking no chances this time, and declared his death some time around 6:51 a.m.

Witnesses tried to rush from the room, many with hands cupped over their mouths and noses, but all were forced to sign an official death certificate before leaving. Oliver A. Jenkins, the Erie County sheriff, had tears in his eyes as he left Kemmler's smoking corpse behind.

At 6:52, in the telegraph center that had been crudely thrown together across the street at the New York Central Railroad station, the first tap of a telegraph set off a torrent of clicks as reporters wired the news all over the world.

In the prison, Alfred P. Southwick did not finish the victory speech he'd started some fifteen minutes prior. Just as he knew Thomas Edison would accept the news, the inventor of the electric chair knew this was a vicious defeat. Despite a legal mandate limiting the press from reporting details on the execution, Southwick knew word would spread like fire. Both the electric chair and alternating current would be seen as failures, severely harming their public reputation and perception.

Numerous doctors, including Dr. Spitzka, later claimed they were certain the first jolt had killed Kemmler. Although Southwick considered the execution a great success (though he'd admit the initial charge should have been left on longer), he knew this was a blaze he could not contain on his own.

Alfred P. Southwick, the dentist-turned-executioner, desperately hoped Thomas Edison had the means to extinguish the bonfire before it destroyed all they had worked so hard to create.

14 IN KEMMLER'S WAKE

In modern times, social media allows the immediate broadcast of news and an equally immediate reaction from the masses. Unlike in the late 1800s, today there is no wait time needed for the facts to be gathered, the report to be written, the article to be printed, and the publication to be distributed by hand. News circulated much slower in the late nineteenth century. But the news of Kemmler's botched electrocution spread swiftly, finding its way into every major publication within hours, and the days that followed brought forth reactions from all sides.

George Westinghouse's statement was one of understandable horror. "It has been a brutal affair," he said publicly, though one can't be sure if he was referring to the execution as "brutal," or the entire back-and-forth battle between himself and Edison. Perhaps he meant both. "They could have done better with an ax." Historians would later debate whether Westinghouse intentionally tied the death to Kemmler's mode of murder by mentioning an ax. After all, Kemmler was known as the "hatchet fiend" to the general public. "My predictions have been verified," Westinghouse added. "The public will lay the blame where it belongs and it will not be on us. I regard the manner of the killing as a complete vindication of all our claims."

Bourke Cockran, Kemmler's defense lawyer, echoed the sentiments of Westinghouse: "It is a sort of ghastly triumph for me. The experts against me on the trial figured it all out that such a shocking thing [an electric execution gone horribly wrong] was impossible and yet it has just happened." Cockran wrongly predicted that "no other state will adopt the electrical execution law." Ohio would later adopt the method as common practice in 1896, followed by Massachusetts in 1898. By 1913, twelve states had adopted the electric chair for capital punishment. That total would rise to twenty-six by 1949 when West Virginia joined the group.

In contrast to Cockran and Westinghouse, dentist Alfred P. Southwick viewed the first electrical execution as a great success. Sure, he admitted, this particular execution had had some problems. But, he reasoned, that was to be expected, given the fact that this was the maiden voyage of the chair. "I tell you," Southwick said to reporters, "this is a grand thing, and is destined to become the system of legal death throughout the world." His words, in retrospect, were surprisingly prophetic.

Thomas Edison understood the press—he'd had ample experience with it over the years—and he knew how the news would be received by the public. Using his tactful approach, Edison responded to the *New York Times* at his home in Llewellyn Park, New Jersey, by stating he wished not to discuss the particulars until he had had time to review the reports. That gave him some time to craft a reply. Once he did respond, Edison explained—with a calm and composed demeanor—that Kemmler undoubtedly died instantly. He added that the excitement of the moment surely had an effect on those in charge of the execution process, and on witnesses. With his signature confidence, he claimed that the next to die in the chair would do so without incident.

Nikola Tesla, unlike the others, could not be reached for immediate comment. After a year working with Westinghouse in Pittsburgh on alternating current, Tesla had decided to leave the laboratory. Tesla still supported and respected George Westinghouse, but he no longer worked with the Westinghouse team. So when reporters tried to contact him for comment, Nikola Tesla was nowhere to be found. It would not be until some forty years later that Tesla commented that the very idea of electrocution was wrong because "an individual under such conditions, while wholly bereft of the consciousness of the lapse of time, retains a keen sense of pain, and a minute of agony is equivalent to that through all eternity."

In one of the most mysterious disappearances in American history, Harold P. Brown—writer of vehement letters to the editor, experimenter of animal electrocution, and challenger of electric duels—vanished following the execution. Brown was an apparition, appearing from out of nowhere to write the letter to the editor and bring down alternating current and then retreating back to nowhere once he'd accomplished what he'd set out to do.

- - - -

The year leading up to the first execution had included a series of relative victories for Thomas Edison, the first of which was alternating current being termed the "executioner's current."

In early 1889, with the economy tightening on Edison, financiers J. P. Morgan and Anthony J. Drexel proposed a merger between Edison Electric Light Company and Drexel, Morgan and Company. On April 24, 1889, this agreement resulted in the creation of Edison General Electric Company.

More good news followed when the price of copper, which direct current needed an ample supply of to run its system, came down in 1889 after Hyacinth Secretan realized he had misjudged the uniform willpower of the electric world. When the price had been pushed so high, the executives of the electric companies simply refused—across the board—to pay the outrageous price Secretan had hung on his copper monopoly. Edison and the rest of the field had called the copper syndicate's bluff.

Edison's long-standing light bulb patent court case, which essentially charged that every existing incandescent bulb model was owing to his design, was ruled in his favor on October 4 of that year, by Justice Bradley. The United States Circuit Court had considered the case for more than a few years, only to rule that these "patent pirates" had one man—and one design—to thank for any subsequent model: Thomas Edison.

Even with the William Kemmler fiasco at Auburn Prison, Thomas Edison's business was soaring.

■　■　■　■

In a similar manner, George Westinghouse's business boomed in 1890.

Even with alternating current firmly linked to the electric chair, the months that followed the Kemmler debacle were stellar for Westinghouse Electric. In October of that year, Baltimore, Maryland, had come through with the purchase of a six-thousand-light alternating current system, one of the largest to date. Another order was put in for 1,500 lights in two different states, in southern New York and Nebraska. Like dominoes, large orders continued to fall into place for George Westinghouse.

Things had been so good, in fact, that Westinghouse had extended his business interests to electric streetcars and arc lighting, the sales of which also took off that year.

By the end of 1890, Westinghouse Electric Company was bringing in a whopping four million dollars in annual sales.

■　■　■　■

All good things come to an end, they say, and this was no more evident than at the tail end of 1890, when the economy crashed in London, England, threatening a collapse in the US as well.

In mid-November 1890, the world's most prestigious banking house, London-based Baring Brothers & Company, was rumored to be filing for bankruptcy. This panic related to risky Baring Brothers investments with Argentina, which was itself enduring a recession. Although a consortium of prominent banks would band together to create a fund and guarantee the

Barings' debts, the effects in the US were monumental, leading all major investors and creditors to begin calling in their loans. In turn, Edison General Electric and Westinghouse Electric both got caught in the Barings Brothers panic crossfire, forcing both electric pioneers to make drastic moves to save their respective livelihoods.

Edison GE president Henry Villard had his finger on the pulse of the world's economic state and knew that the North American Bank—a major source of Edison capital—had collapsed. Villard quickly discussed a possible merger with Charles Coffin of Thomson-Houston, which had also discussed a possible merger with Westinghouse Electric. Thomas Edison, of course, would hear no talk of a possible merger.

In February 1891, Edison turned to his chief financier, J. P. Morgan, who sided with Edison. "I do not see myself how the two things [Edison Electric and Thomson-Houston] can be brought together," Morgan concluded about the possible merger.

On into 1892, Edison Electric board members urged Thomas Edison to consider switching to alternating current. Villard broke it down in monetary terms, suggesting that the amount of money lost when sticking to the long-distance direct current system was crippling them financially. Edison was a stubborn mule who wouldn't budge, no matter how much Villard and the others tried to convince him.

Then, on February 5, 1892, Thomas Edison was told by his personal secretary, Alfred O. Tate, that the merger was going to go through. "His complexion naturally was pale," Tate later said in his memoirs, "a clear healthy paleness, but following my announcement it turned as white as his collar."

In the end, post-merger Edison shareholders controlled even less of the company than Thomson-Houston. Thomas Edison had lost so much he held only 10 percent of Edison General Electric Company stock, putting him in a precarious situation. Edison made claims that he had grown tired of the business and could not "waste my time over electric-lighting matters" because he had "a lot more new material on which to work." His statements painted the picture of a man who wanted to lower his stock in the company, not of a man who had lost so much in his battle with Westinghouse and his stubborn stance to stick with DC. Edison had not only lost control of his company, but the company itself lost Edison's name, changing from Edison General Electric to simply General Electric.

Edison himself, the consummate showman, put on a proud face, claiming he was on board with the merger, while also claiming electricity wasn't his only concern. "Electric lights are too old for me," Edison stated. The great wizard stayed on and championed direct current, for he had vested so much in and fought so hard for the system, but his marginalization bruised his pride, along with his wallet.

George Westinghouse was not immune to the Baring Brothers panic. Upon the first report of the Baring Brothers rumors, Westinghouse immediately sat down and ran the numbers, determining he needed half a million dollars to pay off his creditors and retain Westinghouse Electric. Westinghouse approached his own stockholders to raise the money needed, but the great panic was so strong the effort fell short of reaching the magic number. He was ever the cherished boss, and a group of his employees came together and offered to work for half wages until the crisis had been averted. Westinghouse, proud of his company for the gesture, declined the offer.

The next course of action was to appeal to the prominent bankers in his home city of Pittsburgh and ask them to stand with him at this critical time. When the committee of bankers heard his pleas, Westinghouse showed his sense of confidence that the crisis would pass by offering his mansion, which he called "Solitude," as collateral. The committee agreed to review the proposal and go over the figures at once.

Then, on December 10, the board of directors of Westinghouse Electric agreed to raise the required half million by creating and selling preferred stock. In the successive days, a slew of businessmen and banks offered up varying amounts of funds, and traded for stock at an inflated price. All seemed well, until a rogue banker decided George Westinghouse was on the ropes and suggested they had the opportunity to seize operating control of the company due to the inventor's dire state. Westinghouse, though, simply said that was impossible. Then he got up, smiled at the collection of moneymen, told a few jokes, thanked them for their consideration and time, and left. This was *his* company. That would never change, not while he still lived and breathed.

In 1891, Westinghouse continued to turn over all stones to

solve his looming financial dependency. When he met August Belmont, of Wall Street investment house August Belmont & Company, Westinghouse believed he might have found a match. The tentative plan that was proposed with Belmont involved selling a chunk of stock by having existing shareholders turn in 40 percent of their stock and accept a much lower value, and then turning around and paying the greedy creditors with the new preferred stock. This would work, Westinghouse knew, but one stipulation remained that might ruin the deal. According to the terms, Westinghouse had to eliminate "doubtful values and the book value of patents." In the end, the major issue was Nikola Tesla's patent royalty deal, which was sucking vast sums of money from the company.

Though he'd remained in contact and advised Westing-house Electric whenever possible, Nikola Tesla had been away from the Pittsburgh lab for more than a year, spending most of his time living in hotels and eating out, habits that would remain a constant for the rest of his life. He'd traveled to Europe, met with experts in many fields of science, and then returned to New York, where he started a new labora-tory on Fifth Avenue, dipping his toes into many different electric experiments, including a protofluorescent bulb that was filament- and wire-free. His wealth from his Westing-house deal had afforded him to live a life that was essentially free of material want and spend money carelessly, knowing his deal would continue to churn out profits throughout his life.

In early 1891, George Westinghouse paid a visit to Tesla's lab. After hearing about and seeing Tesla's latest discoveries, his old boss shared the news about the company's financial crisis. In Westinghouse's signature no-nonsense mode, he inquired with Tesla about the possibility of terminating his AC patent contract and waiving his present and future royalties.

Tesla asked what would happen if he refused, to which Westinghouse said he would lose control of the company to the banks. It would no longer be his company to run.

"If I give up the contract," Tesla said, "you will save your company and retain control? You will proceed with your plans to give my polyphase system to the world?"

Westinghouse nodded and did him one better, telling the Serbian genius what he would do even if he lost control of the company. "I believe your polyphase system is the greatest discovery in the field of electricity . . . I intend to continue, no matter what happens, to proceed with my original plans to put the country on an alternating current basis."

Nikola Tesla, seeing the future of alternating current hanging in the balance, didn't hesitate in weighing the value of financial gain against the survival and utilization of his alternating current system.

"The benefits that will come to civilization from my polyphase system mean more to me than the money involved." Tesla stood and grinned at his friend. Then he held up two documents. "Here is your contract and here is my contract—I will tear both of them to pieces and you will no longer have any troubles from my royalties." Nikola Tesla had given up a fortune to see his vision—his flash of light—become a reality.

In July 1891—with Tesla's contract no longer an issue—a new board was organized to help stabilize Westinghouse Electric & Manufacturing Company, with George Westinghouse in operational control. He had done it.

15 | ALL THE WORLD'S A STAGE

During the Gilded Age, the world was beginning to come together in terms of communication. Improvements to the telegraph and the advent of the telephone allowed people to communicate over long distances. Postal carriers and railways allowed items to be delivered across the country with more ease than in the past. News communication via telegraph allowed current events to be disseminated in various print publications more easily than in previous decades. But even with these new innovations, the world of the late 1800s was nothing like it is today, where the average citizen can immediately connect with anyone else anywhere on the globe.

One major event that united people from different countries all over was called the world's fair. Held every few years, the tradition can be credited to the French, who would routinely put on national exhibitions that featured the best the nation had to offer related to a specific theme, like the 1844 Industrial Exhibition in Paris, which focused on the most exciting industrial and technological developments in the country. This tradition spread to a worldwide fair, which moved from one nation to another, with different themes. Each was like a worldwide all-star extravaganza that revolved around the given theme.

These world's fairs, with the collection of esteemed people from so many nations, served as *the* place to show off whatever was new and exciting. It was the only way, in fact, to display an innovation for a diverse audience at one given time. In a way, the world's fairs of the past were like today's internet because they showcased a device to widely disparate eyes at one time.

In 1893, a new world's fair was coming to the United States, and dignitaries from all over would be in Chicago, Illinois, for what was being called the World's Columbian Exposition. Of course, with electricity as the most prominent of sciences of the time, inventors and businessmen knew that gaining the right to power the World's Columbian Exposition in Chicago would be the ultimate showcase of their system. This set up a showdown between Westinghouse and AC, and General Electric and DC. Whichever company could win the contract to power the new world's fair would have the attention of all the most important people in the world. The ultimate stage had welcomed our key players.

■　■　■　■

May 16, 1892
Rookery Building, Chicago, Illinois

All eyes stared at the iron box atop the long, sturdy table. The box was black and had been polished to a dull sheen. It had no markings or decoration. Just a large box, it appeared, so plain and unassuming that it would seem nothing of value could be contained within. But that was far from the truth, since inside were the bids from General Electric and Westinghouse Electric to light and power the upcoming 1893 World's Fair in Chicago.

A key hung in the cigar-smoke-thickened air, the peering eyes so focused on the jagged item that the hand holding it might as well have been invisible. The key dropped down to the box, cutting the smoke and silence as it moved. Half the key disappeared with an echoing *click*. The key turned and then stopped with a second *click*.

Silence.

Two hands captured everyone's focus, one hand holding the side of the black box, the other slowly lifting the hinged door, opening it wide.

A deep voice announced that there were two bids.

The captivated eyes around the room followed the hands as they dropped down and disappeared inside the box and then reappeared with two small envelopes.

Nervous chattering and murmuring beat down the silence.

The first bid belonged to General Electric, explained the deep voice—the owner of the attention-grabbing hands, Daniel H. Burnham, the Chicago World's Fair's director of works. The middle-aged man looked around the room at the hypnotized audience and then announced the bid, which came in at $554,000.

The nervous chattering returned, along with a few short laughs, as this bid was nothing compared to the first one General Electric had issued less than two months prior. That offer, though, had come when there had been no serious competition. But things had changed.

Burnham made it known that the other envelope contained the Westinghouse Electric bid. With a slight grin, Burnham announced the Westinghouse bid of $399,000, concluding that the contract was awarded to Westinghouse.

Captain Eugene Griffin, second vice president of General Electric, shot to his feet. With balled fists and a set jaw, Griffin reminded Burnham about an important matter: the Edison light bulb patent litigation. As everyone was aware, the injunction was all but certain to be ruled in General Electric's favor. What wasn't set in stone was whether the ruling would mandate that General Electric would still be forced to sell its bulbs to Westinghouse and other companies. Griffin made it clear that once the case had been decided, GE would no longer sell bulbs to Westinghouse Electric, making it unwise for Fair officials to award the contract to Westinghouse.

Burnham got lost in a huddle of quick-talking men, all with their heads shaking and hands moving wildly. These fellow Committee on Grounds and Buildings members seized the director of works and took shelter in a locked room to discuss the matter discreetly before committing to a decision.

George Westinghouse caught the eye of his friend Charles Terry. Westinghouse nodded. This was not surprising. At every turn Thomas Edison had thwarted Westinghouse's sale and promotion of alternating current, and now Charles Coffin—the new president of General Electric—had taken up the same charge. Terry nodded back at Westinghouse. They both knew Westinghouse had made a low and enticing offer, one which would barely—if at all—result in profit. But it was an offer the committee wouldn't be able to refuse, and it was an opportunity to gain something even more valuable than financial profit: it would allow their electrical system to be seen by all. Not just those in the electric fraternity, and not just those in the US, but people from all over the world. You couldn't put a price tag on that kind of publicity and exposure.

Confident but anxious, George Westinghouse stood up when the committee reappeared at seven p.m. to inform their eager audience that they would need more time to decide. Burnham told both sides they would be consulting their team of lawyers and would be in touch when they had made a decision, leaving the latest battle undecided. For now.

George Westinghouse nodded again. The World's Columbian Exposition was meant to signify the four hundredth anniversary of Christopher Columbus's arrival in America, and at the same time showcase the industrial and cultural might of the world. This was the perfect setting to display the safe and effective alternating current system, and George Westinghouse was not about to have the door slammed in his face, especially after he had almost missed the opportunity to begin with.

■ ■ ■ ■

Less than two months prior, on April 2, 1892, the same iron box had also featured two bids. One had been the Charles Coffin–issued General Electric bid of a whopping $1,720,000, while the other had come from a small Chicago-based businessman named Charles F. Locksteadt, who had submitted a relatively minuscule $625,600 offer on behalf of South Side Machine and Metal Works.

Mere numbers indicated the Locksteadt bid was significantly better than the lofty General Electric figure, but the major hang-up was as substantial as the difference between the two bids: Charles F. Locksteadt was a relative nobody in the electrical field; his name didn't inspire any confidence that he could actually follow through with such an undertaking.

All along, Charles Coffin knew he had the Fair's board of directors where he wanted them, as the new Edison-free General Electric "trustification" held leverage over every other struggling business in the field, thanks in large part to the economic panic that had forced Thomas Edison to lose control of his business with the Thomson-Houston merger.

George Westinghouse, in fact, had just battled for more than a year to maintain control of his own company, which was the main reason he had steered clear of putting forth an offer. By the time Westinghouse had held on to his business and established Westinghouse Electric & Manufacturing Company, the World's Fair bids had already been submitted.

Charles Coffin knew Westinghouse had missed the window to compete for the Fair—or so he thought—leaving him more than comfortable to issue such a massive bid. As a sign of how much had changed in the last half year, when the World's Fair officials had bargained with Chicago Edison in October 1891 for arc lights to use for construction, they had settled on a price of $11.00 per arc light. Now, only six months later, Coffin and the General Electric crew had raised their price tag to $38.50.

When Fair officials had opened the iron box for that first time on April 2, they had begun considering the two offers. No immediate decision was made, which suggested they were not completely sold on either offer. Charles F. Locksteadt sensed he had a chance, and he quickly approached George Westinghouse about teaming up. This was a second chance for Westinghouse— a new window of opportunity had opened for him.

Upon Westinghouse's acceptance to team up with Locksteadt, World's Fair president Harlow Higinbotham decided to reset the bidding and begin anew for all concerned, leading to the second reveal of the iron box—a second round of bids that was now going before a team of lawyers, keeping both sides of the war on edge.

■　■　■　■

May 23, 1892
Rookery Building, Chicago, Illinois

George Westinghouse set down his black umbrella beside his chair. He ran his open palms over his dark formal suit, making sure he was presentable. He gazed down at the large table, which looked almost identical to the way it had looked a week ago. This time, though, there was no iron box arresting everyone's attention.

Westinghouse sat down and addressed the familiar company

with his eyes. He nodded at his friend Charles Terry just as he had a week prior. The telegram that had beckoned him the day before had led to his half-day journey from Pittsburgh to Chicago aboard his private railcar, the Glen Eyre. Now it was time to hear the verdict.

Chicago World's Fair director of works Daniel H. Burnham addressed his audience, explaining that after due consideration they had decided to bestow the contract on Westinghouse Electric. But, Burnham quickly added, they were going to split the contract in two.

George Westinghouse shook his head. No, he explained, that would not do. He had presented the lowest bid, and now, he concluded, his "first-class apparatus" should be granted the entire job. He ran his fingers over his signature muttonchop facial hair. Then he made it clear he felt he should be given the entire contract.

Burnham's eyes moved from one committee member to the next. They were speechless.

GE's second vice president Captain Griffin smirked, bringing up the light bulb patent lawsuit again. Westinghouse had a strong bluff, but Griffin knew he had the legal threat stashed away in his hand. To Griffin, his card trumped Westinghouse's.

Once again Burnham and the committee retreated to a private room, coming out soon after to ask George Westinghouse a direct and loaded question: Would he and Westinghouse Electric put up a one-million-dollar bond guaranteeing the contract, even if the light bulb matter didn't fall in their favor?

Westinghouse nodded without hesitation. He explained that they had already moved in a direction that no longer relied on Edison and General Electric's bulbs. He didn't show any signs of anxiety about the fact that he'd have to front five hundred thousand dollars for the one-million-dollar bond.

Burnham and the board members met privately again, not surfacing until seven thirty p.m. Burnham announced that Westinghouse had gained the contract as he approached the satisfied man with an extended arm and an open hand. Smiles were exchanged as hands shook on the agreement, with signed contracts to follow.

Captain Griffin and his General Electric representatives rushed to the door. In a huff, Griffin made it clear that once the courts had ruled in their favor, Westinghouse would "not be able to make his own lamps . . . we will not let him continue his contract."

Griffin made his dramatic exit and all eyes returned to George Westinghouse for a reply. The confident man didn't feel it necessary to address Griffin's threat, saying only that Westinghouse Electric had already come to a resolution for the light bulb problem. Instead of detailing this resolution, he turned to the members of the press in attendance and said, "I shall put in ten or twelve dynamos of 12,000 lamp capacity and furnish a clean-cut, first-class system. I have about 100,000 lamps, either completed or partly so, at the works, and there will be no difficulty in furnishing material. I am required to have between 5,000 and 10,000 lamps installed by the 1st of October. This is an easy task."

But it *wasn't* an easy task, and George Westinghouse knew it. He had secured the cherished contract, but now he essentially had to design machinery for an entirely new system of electrical operation and construct a new light bulb that didn't infringe on Edison's patent, and he needed to do this in just over one calendar year.

May 25, 1892
Westinghouse Machine Shop, Pittsburgh, Pennsylvania

"How soon may I have four of them?"

That was George Westinghouse's question to his lead draftsman, E. S. McClelland. The day before, after he had made the journey back from Chicago to Pittsburgh overnight aboard the Glen Eyre, Westinghouse had shared the news with his crew that they would be in charge of lighting and powering the Chicago World's Fair, which was less than a year away. He had asked his team to design a 1,200 brake horsepower engine that operated at 200 revolutions per minute, 150 pounds per square inch boiler pressure, with splash lubrication. And not to be ignored, one that had to fit in a limited amount of space.

For the next twenty-four hours, McClelland and his team had designed—in sketch form—an engine that met the specifications. And to accommodate the space limitations, they had decided to make it a vertical engine after they had turned the drawing on its side while looking it over.

Westinghouse's question wasn't so much a question; it was an imperative handed off to his team. Rephrased, their encouraging yet demanding boss meant: "This will work perfectly. Now get right to it and put four of them together without delay."

· · · ·

As the summer of 1892 continued, so too did preparations for the 1893 World's Fair. At the same time, a collection of near seven thousand workers continued their efforts to transform a swampy six-hundred-acre area of Chicago into a magnificent landscape envisioned by Frederick Law Olmsted. To add to the busy nature of Fair preparations, George Westinghouse was working on the challenging task of lighting and running the exposition with alternating current.

Alternating current machinery, though, wasn't all that had to be created. No, George Westinghouse also had to prepare as if the Edison light bulb patent was going to be upheld, which meant he needed to design and manufacture over 92,000 bulbs that didn't yet exist.

Westinghouse wasn't all bark when it came to his word that he had been preparing as if they'd need a completely new bulb. In fact, for the last few months he had dipped into his old patents and began work on a Sawyer-Man "stopper" light, one that featured a two-piece design that Westinghouse felt would easily differentiate it from Edison's one-piece bulb. He had purchased the patents from inventors William Sawyer and Albon Man, and he held exclusive rights to manufacture and sell lamps that used the design. But first he had to modify the design to make it practical. Months of experimentation led to small successes followed by ultimate failures. Throughout the process, the Westinghouse team learned from their mistakes and continued to make progress.

Toward the end of 1892, Westinghouse reached the point where the lamp was functional and nearly ready to mass-produce. The design included an iron-and-glass "stopper" that was fit snugly into the glass globe, allowing it to be opened and the filament replaced once it burned out.

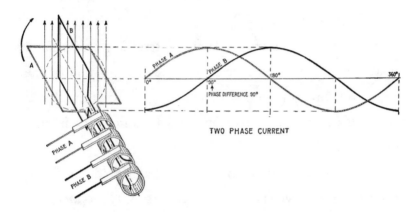

Two-phase alternating current

The Edison light bulb patent was upheld on October 4, 1892, followed a month later by a federal court ruling that Westinghouse was no longer allowed to make Edison-style lamps, and then punctuated by the December 15 denial to an appeal, making the litigation final. At long last, the light bulb war had been settled.

But the War of the *Currents* waged on.

For George Westinghouse, losing the light bulb ruling simply meant his "stopper" lamp had to succeed, which led to his swift decision to transform a portion of the Westinghouse Air Brake Company in Allegheny, Pennsylvania, into a glass and light bulb factory fully dedicated to mass-producing the new bulbs.

General Electric representatives continued their attempts at hindering Westinghouse by filing a last-ditch restraining order that they hoped would prohibit the production of the Sawyer-Man "stopper" bulbs, claiming this new design, too, infringed on the Edison patent.

Westinghouse caught wind of the restraining order and had his lawyers present and prepared at the hearing, and the new year of 1893 brought with it a final, concluding ruling that the Sawyer-Man "stopper" patent was indeed unique, no infringement present.

The courtroom was no longer a battlefield for George Westinghouse. Now all that remained was mass-producing over 100,000 bulbs, all the while designing and then actually building alternating current machinery that was ten times more powerful than anything in existence.

George Westinghouse needed help.

■ ■ ■ ■

Nikola Tesla became a regular presence in the Allegheny factory at the beginning of 1893.

Tesla and Westinghouse immediately settled back into their comfortable relationship built on trust and respect, deciding that they should place "two single phase alternators side by side, with their armature windings staggered 90 degrees," in order to achieve Tesla's two-phase AC design, which would soon be featured on all Tesla induction motors. When they had completed their work, each piece of machinery had the capability of powering just over thirty thousand "stopper" lamps.

In the January 1893 issue of *Electrical Engineer*, it was reported that there were twelve nearly completed vertical generators that operated 1,000-horsepower engines weighing seventy-five tons apiece. The article concluded that it would "constitute the largest single exhibit of operating machinery ever made at any exposition, and probably the most extensive exhibit in the Fair." Of course, there was still much work to be done, but the report assured Fair officials that the exposition was on schedule, while at the same time it infuriated General Electric representatives, who had exhausted their efforts to thwart Westinghouse's success.

As insurance, Westinghouse decided that each generator would have its own backup generator, keeping the World's Fair constantly powered. There would be no unexpected blackouts; Tesla and Westinghouse made sure of that. All told, everything would be powered by a massive 2,000-horsepower Allis-Chalmers engine, and everything would be fueled with oil, eliminating the smoky grime that came with coal.

Work continued from winter to spring, accompanied by glitches and hang-ups. In the end, most of the machinery and all the bulbs were on the Chicago fairgrounds mere weeks before opening day. They'd gotten everything delivered, but just under the wire.

Still, the task wasn't to simply have the alternating current machinery *there*. The ultimate goal was to successfully light and power the Fair. Only upon doing so would George Westinghouse have a clear-cut victory in this pivotal battle.

■　■　■　■

May 1, 1893
World's Columbian Exposition, Chicago, Illinois

President Grover Cleveland, casually dressed so as to not steal all the attention on this occasion, stood firm with his hand hovering over a welcoming gold-and-ivory telegraph key. Overhead, glimmering in the suddenly bright daylight of midmorning, the golden dome of the Administration Building sent specks and shards of sunlight in all directions, as if the golden dome were surrounded by a radiant halo.

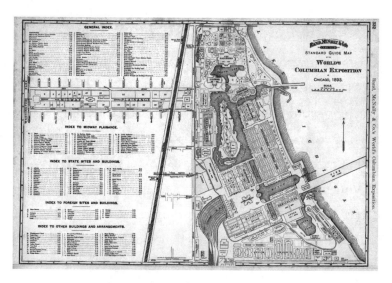

Map of the 1893 World's Columbian Exposition, considered the "World Series" of the AC/DC war

President Cleveland spoke with authority, his voice capturing the many anxious visitors in full arrest. He paused, and the spectators housed under the radiant Administration Building umbrella followed suit, barely a breath taken as Cleveland slowly lowered his finger.

As the tip of Cleveland's index finger met the telegraph key, the silence gave way to a loud and angelic choir who sang "Hallelujah Chorus" with energy that spread from one onlooker to the next. A hum of excitement and wonder rippled over the audience.

And like the energy that spread from the choir to the audience, the impression of the telegraph key spread an electric charge along a long wire some hundreds of feet away to Machinery Hall, where Westinghouse engineers and workers waited much like the crowd had moments before—silent, in full arrest. After all, this was the moment of truth.

Westinghouse dynamo in Machinery Hall, 1893 World's Columbian Exposition

They watched the massive Allis-Chalmers engine, collectively willing it to come to life and ease their nerves.

And it did.

The 2,000-horsepower monster surged with electricity, immediately pumping power into the arteries of the many Westinghouse generators. Quickly, the generators seized this new energy and spread it through the veins of wires in all directions around the fairgrounds.

In the Court of Honor—dubbed the "White City" due to the architecture's consistency of white plaster and "staff" (artificial stone) all around—three fountains shot streams of water into the air, signaling to Westinghouse engineers and fairgoers alike that the Fair now had been powered up with alternating current.

1893 World's Columbian Exposition, Court of Honor

Statue of the Republic, 1893 World's Columbian Exposition

In the Court of Honor and onstage at the gold-domed Administration Building, as well as back in Machinery Hall, cheers and applause and whoops mixed together in harmony with the boat whistles, cannon fire, foghorns, and bells that moved in waves over the Grand Basin. As flags from the many represented countries unfurled all along the Court of Honor, the boisterous mixture of celebratory sounds came together in the middle of the Grand Basin's giant pool of water, where the "Statue of the Republic" stood with raised hands—a globe topped with a spread-winged eagle in her right hand, a staff in her left hand, topped by a laurel-encircled plaque engraved with the word "Liberty."

Thus, despite the fact that more than a few attractions had yet to be opened to the public, the 1893 Columbian Exposition had officially been launched by George Westinghouse. His alternating current system was now powering the entire Fair.

The cold and rainy weather that had led up to opening day returned on day two and lingered for most of that first week. This nasty weather, in conjunction with the delayed opening of various attractions, didn't hurt attendance. Over the six-month span of the entire exposition, over twenty-seven million visitors from all over the world would pay the fifty-cent admission fee to see a host of sights they'd never seen before.

There was George Washington Ferris's Wheel, 250 feet high with thirty-six cabin cars spread out in equally spaced fashion. Then there was the Intramural Elevated Railway, which shuttled visitors from one place to another; the very first moving sidewalk, which spanned some three thousand feet along the pier; and various machines of the Libby Glass Company. There was also the electric kitchen in Jackson Park, which showcased the many state-of-the-art devices being introduced to the public, and each and every one was made possible—and operational—by Westinghouse Electric and its efficient and safe alternating current.

George Washington Ferris's Wheel, 1893 World's Columbian Exposition

Yes, everything was given life by the system that Harold P. Brown had spent so much time tearing down and forcing the public to see as the "executioner's current." Now, as person after person attended the Fair and saw, firsthand and up close, that this system of electricity was far from deadly, the lens through which the public saw alternating current had been changed. With the uninterrupted availability and the accident- and incident-free track record as days wore on, people began to see alternating current as a harmless, do-it-all method of powering the world.

But George Westinghouse and his team had made sure this event was flawless, so they weren't surprised by their success. In fact, although he had been commissioned for 92,000 bulbs, to make sure the lights would never go out—or even dim in the slightest—Westinghouse had come to the table with 250,000 bulbs to use at the exposition. Daily, 180,000 bulbs found use, leaving a rather healthy reserve of 70,000-plus bulbs. George Westinghouse had extensively planned for problems, and he had accommodated for the fact that there *would* be problems. Like, for example, a multitude of burned-out bulbs. As an added safeguard, Westinghouse employed a team of workers whose sole job encompassed running around the park to deliver and change bulbs whenever necessary.

And when it came to the wire and cable that fed electricity all over the park, Westinghouse and Burnham had wisely decided to bury everything in a wide subway-style tunnel system that afforded the ability to discreetly access and fix any faulty wiring.

There were 1,560 manholes all around the grounds, making it convenient to gain access just about anywhere. This underground series of tunnels also allowed the wires that the public had begun to associate with danger to be out of sight, taking the threat and fear of live wires away from passersby.

The safety of the wire-free environment allowed fairgoers to feel at ease and unthreatened by the constant presence of electricity all around them. With this comfortability, visitors checked out the many items and inventions being introduced to the public for the first time.

And there was much to be seen, as the 1893 World's Fair held many brand-new inventions that would end up becoming staples of America's future, including the zipper, Cracker Jack, Wrigley's Juicy Fruit gum, spray paint, the dishwasher, and Aunt Jemima pancake mix.

With all the attractions to visit, what impressed people most might have been the display of electric power throughout the Fair. This shouldn't have come as a surprise, simply based on the numbers. Compared to the previous World's Fair, in 1889 in Paris, where 3,000 horsepower had been employed, the 1893 Columbian Exposition pumped out a whopping 29,000 horsepower. In fact, the *Review of Reviews* concluded, "The World's Fair probably comes as near being the electrician's ideal city as any spot on the globe."

It was at night, though, that the Chicago World's Fair enraptured fairgoers. As day gave way to day and word spread, it became known that the daytime hours were nothing compared to the prime time that was sunset and nighttime. Each day as the sun disappeared over the horizon, the brilliance of the White City mystified man and child alike.

The Administration Building at the 1893 World's Columbian Exposition, completely powered and lit up by AC

Without fail, it'd grow silent as the sky grew dark, people waiting in earnest, staring at their surroundings. As it began, the gold-domed Administration Building lit up like a mushroom on fire, followed by the white buildings all around the Court, which were riddled with bulbs that went off one after another like silent fireworks. Thousands of bluish arc lights lined the walkways all over the grounds, while gondolas and boats in the Basin added to the light extravaganza with bobbing, rocking bulbs that flicked on at night. Then there was the Ferris Wheel, covered with three thousand lights, rotating slowly like a grounded moon engulfed in flames.

Then, from the highest rooftops, four huge searchlights shone different-colored lights into the black sky. Green, red, white, and blue barbs of light danced in the air. The colors changed in uniform fashion to the delight of the audience, who *ooh*ed and *ahh*ed. As if that wasn't enough, every night soon after the searchlights lit up the sky with the colorful light show, everything went dark once again. From bright light all over to sudden . . .

Darkness.

People all around turned their attention to the darkened Basin, where the MacMonnies fountain loomed. Murmurs and whispers from the crowd could be heard as "the great electric fountains lifted their gushing and gleaming waters . . . one on either side of the MacMonnies fountain, and through all their many changes each was the counterpart of the other, alike in color and form." Different lines and shapes and colors came together in the spraying water as people stood in awe.

For the first month of operation, as new attractions slowly opened almost daily, people rushed to the Fair to pay witness to the power of the White City. And each night at nine thirty p.m. when the Fair closed, people left with a smile on their faces, eyes wide in disbelief.

But it was one month into the Fair's existence that the *true* draw of the exposition opened: the Electricity Building.

Electricity Building, 1893 World's Columbian Exposition

On June 1, 1893, amid a steady downpour, people flocked to the newly opened Electricity Building. Everyone wanted a glimpse inside this crystal ball of the technological future.

Just outside the entrance, visitors were welcomed by an enormous statue of Benjamin Franklin, all decked out in full colonial garb, his historic kite in hand.

Inside, a three-acre exhibition hall was lit up with thirty

thousand bulbs, which forced fairgoers to adjust their eyes to the brilliant display. Flags and ceremonial bunting lined the second-story balcony all around the hall, the colorful drapery catching the light in welcoming fashion.

Once their eyes adjusted to the bright light, people rushed from exhibition to exhibition, each attraction even better than the one before.

And though the 1893 World's Fair was powered by George Westinghouse's alternating current, Charles Coffin had made sure the Electricity Building was teeming with all things Edison, including an eighty-foot Columbian column covered with hundreds of Edison light fixtures. Atop this column was an eight-foot-tall half-ton Edison bulb shining with sparkling magnificence through some five thousand small prisms. In rhythm and time with the music playing in the hall, the lights changed colors and twinkled as though the column itself were moving and interacting with the music. A less-than-subtle jab at Westinghouse was made in the fact that the full seven-volume, seven-thousand-page record of the light bulb case was at the base of the column for everyone to read at their leisure.

Charles Coffin and General Electric used Edison's name to remind fairgoers of General Electric's presence, since even though Edison's name had been removed from the company's title and banner, everyone still associated Thomas Edison with the GE brand.

As such, Thomas Edison's Kinetoscope was featured as well,

the new invention that displayed the first motion pictures. On the screen of the Kinetoscope, Prime Minister William Gladstone of Great Britain delivered a speech in the House of Commons, forcing people to do a double take at the reality that this was only a recorded production and not the real thing.

The main floor of the Electricity Building drew excited visitors in droves, as the major inventors of the time were present to display their latest discoveries. Front and center, headlining the inventor docket was none other than Nikola Tesla.

One display that impressed those in the electric fraternity more than the average person was the Tesla/Westinghouse model of the alternating current system, which covered a long table. While the common man and woman walked right past without a glance, the electricians and inventors in attendance stopped and studied the intricate detail spread out on the table, as if they were staring at a scene from the future through a time machine.

Tesla AC model demonstration, 1893 World's Columbian Exposition

Electricity Building, 1893 World's Columbian Exposition

Nikola Tesla himself was a hot-ticket item. The Serbian immigrant dressed to impress. For this show he had an ostrich-sized copper egg surrounded by an array of smaller copper eggs which served as planets, a simulation of the Milky Way galaxy on display. Just as the onlookers began to nod and clap, the eccentric inventor let them know this was just the beginning.

For his next act, Nikola Tesla took to a darkened room with a crackling "Westinghouse" sign lit up and pulsing with energy just outside the entryway. Thunder boomed inside the dark room as two rubber plates lined with tinfoil—about fifteen feet apart, serving as terminals—hung suspended above the gaunt inventor. When the current was turned on, empty bulbs and tubes around the room lit up. These bulbs were not connected to wires and seemingly not connected to the terminals, yet they were illuminated just the same. In various areas of the dark room, glass tubing lit up and formed the names of famous electricians, Tesla's way of paying homage to his esteemed colleagues. Excluding Thomas Edison, of course. Amid the glowing tubes, sparks and daggers of light blanketed the aluminum-covered surface all around the "electrified" room.

These two acts became regular features at the Fair, satisfying all who witnessed them. But what everyone *really* wanted to see—what they'd heard about in mythical manner—was how the great Nikola Tesla could pass electricity through his body without being harmed. It was something he'd done in Paris years prior, and word had spread that he was aiming to do it again at the Fair.

August 25, 1893
World's Columbian Exposition, Chicago, Illinois

Over a thousand electrical engineers and scientists along with a host of common fairgoers crammed into Assembly Hall in the Agricultural Building. Today was the day, and the hour was upon them. Nikola Tesla was about to pass 250,000 volts of current through his body.

Inventor Elisha Gray stood on a platform and addressed the crowd and introduced Tesla as the "Wizard of Physics," handing over the stage to the guest of honor.

Nikola Tesla addressed the eager onlookers. He was standing on a platform wearing a tailored four-button brown suit. To his sides were small cylinders of heavy steel mounted on steel pedestals, each held up by an insulated wooden base. A wooden table was to one side of Tesla, small electrical appliances stacked and piled up high.

Tesla joked about his frail frame and informed the audience he was about to lecture on "Mechanical and Electrical Oscillators." He detailed the fact that oscillators could transmit information or electric energy and he could create pulsations through objects of various kinds. He then explained that he had designed steam generators that were so small he could fit them in a derby hat.

Then talk gave way to action. Tesla knew it was time to mystify the audience.

Without delay, Tesla made objects light up, spark, and seemingly glow with electric flame, and he lit up protofluorescent lights of varying sizes and shapes. The crowd watched with delight.

With a flourish, Tesla engulfed himself in a pool of pulsating light that passed in waves around his body. Tesla was surrounded by a storm of white flame. The current of light subsided and Tesla stood for the successive minutes amid a halo of sparking light that seemed to cling to his brown suit.

What the public didn't quite understand was that Nikola Tesla was never really in danger. He understood the science of electricity, and this knowledge is what kept him safe. The alternating current that flowed from the oscillator didn't pass through his body but instead traveled around the outside of his gaunt frame. Though it looked like electricity was slicing through Tesla, in reality this high-voltage current was moving along the surface of his skin and his pristine brown suit. His internal organs, like his heart and lungs, were protected by the science that Nikola Tesla understood completely.

After the final sparks danced on the floor like grease on a frying pan, everything stopped. No one moved as that final spark disappeared.

At once, the audience hopped to their feet and let loose in applause. Nikola Tesla bowed gracefully and grinned. The stage was his, and he owned it.

And while Tesla owned the moment, when the Fair closed shop on October 30, George Westinghouse owned the War of the Currents.

Despite their profit of just under twenty thousand dollars, the six months of publicity for alternating current and Westinghouse Electric was priceless. Prior to the exhibition, alternating current had been a stranger to the average citizen, linked to death and danger more than anything else. Now, as the fair came to an end, both alternating current and Westinghouse Electric were welcomed by mainstream society, like trusted friends. George Westinghouse and alternating current had won over the public. Completely.

16 ONE RISES, ONE FALLS

The 1893 World's Columbian Exposition was a major victory for Westinghouse, Tesla, and alternating current, but a war isn't over until one side either surrenders or is no longer standing. Direct current and General Electric—with Thomas Edison barely in the fold—still had their legs beneath them. True, General Electric and direct current might have been wobbly and wounded, but they had some fight left.

Fittingly, the final round of the vicious war of electricity would be fought straddling a line. But unlike most of the battles of the War of the Currents, which had tilted one way or the other on a line separating the ethical from the unethical, this final showdown would take place on a geographical line between the US and Canada: Niagara Falls.

That same natural marvel that had captured a teenage Nikola Tesla upon reading about it and seeing breathtaking images in books was now the setting of the climactic battle in the epic war. That "flash of light" of a giant wheel being turned continually by the powerful water had dominated his mind from adolescence to adulthood. And that vow he had made to his uncle to make that vision a reality was now in focus. It was a chance to make his dream come true.

This battle had actually started years before, in 1886, when Thomas Evershed—Erie Canal engineer—had a magnificent idea after learning of the Niagara Reservation, which was a series of mandates and restrictions passed by the New York State government forbidding any and all man-made waterways on its four-hundred-acre plot of state land. Evershed's mind had focused on the restrictions—the sacred and protected four-hundred-acre limit—and this triggered his idea: the Niagara Project, a plan to capture the natural power of the falls by creating a canal waterwheel power system set up a mile above the falls, keeping it beyond the restricted area.

In sum, his plan was to redirect Niagara River water into a canal that would feed into a complex mill of two hundred water-wheels. After working its way from the river to the canal and through the wheels, the water would be sent down a long tail-race tunnel far underground beneath the town of Niagara. This useful water that'd set the wheels in perpetual motion would travel through the tailrace and then reenter the Niagara downriver of the falls.

But in order for it to be successful, the Niagara Project would require vast sums of money. In fact, some would joke—although it might not have been much of an exaggeration—the amount of capital needed for the project far exceeded the enormity of the Niagara Cataract itself.

Thomas Evershed did not possess the funds needed to see his plan through, so he formed a team to help round up investors. From the outset, the Evershed group had trouble finding moneymen who could actually come through with the funds needed. To help their cause, they enlisted the help of William Rankine, New York attorney and friend to many prominent businessmen.

Rankine immediately tempted investors, but the first few balked at actually putting up the capital needed. Enlisting the resilient and relentless Rankine paid off for the Evershed group, literally, when he landed none other than J. P. Morgan to contribute to the project. This was the same investor who had fronted many leading companies and businesses, including Thomas Edison and General Electric. He was the top dog of investors, and when he got involved that usually meant others followed his lead.

It was Morgan who helped point Rankine and the Evershed group toward the man who'd end up taking over the planning and implementation of the project, a New York investment banker named Edward Dean Adams.

When first approached by Rankine, Morgan initially indicated he had great confidence in the *prospects* of the project, only to decline after meeting with Rankine in person. Rankine was confused. Not wanting to lose this financial powerhouse who could make the Niagara Project a reality, he asked Morgan what he could do to turn that initial interest and confidence into a commitment. Morgan mentioned that he liked the plan and the details but claimed they didn't have anyone in place to run it. When Rankine asked for his opinion on the matter, Morgan flatly said that if they could convince Edward Dean Adams to head the project, he'd be convinced enough to invest. At the tail end of 1889, Adams accepted the position, and Morgan put his money where his mouth was, and another 102 wealthy, respected investors also put up $2,630,000 to officially create the Cataract Construction Company.

To help him plan and construct the entire operation, Adams brought aboard Coleman Sellers, an experienced and respected mechanical engineer from Philadelphia. Additionally, Adams enlisted the services of Scottish mathematician Sir William Thomson to head the newly formed International Niagara Commission, charged with the task of determining the best and most efficient way to utilize the power of the falls.

While the use of a long underground tailrace was quickly decided upon unanimously, members of the commission debated internally over how, exactly, they should use the falls to fully realize its most effective power potential. Much like the electric fraternity itself, there was a split between which system would work best: direct or alternating current.

In the early fall of 1890, Thomson and the International Niagara Commission invited engineers from around the world to submit packaged solution plans for the best way to harness Niagara's energy. They advertised that they'd award "prizes" for proposals, the highest amount being three thousand dollars.

Fourteen proposals later—with George Westinghouse

adamantly refusing to supply "free" information without any true motivation—the commission continued to weigh the options while the physical construction got started.

Beginning with the tailrace, ground was broken on October 4, 1890, as 1,300 men made use of dynamite to dent the ground, pickaxes and sledgehammers to chip and break it up, and mules to trudge shards of rock and gravel to wagons that wheeled away unwanted debris from the tailrace site. Work continued around the clock day in and day out. Adams and Sellers adjusted their plans a few months into the project, shortening the tailrace from the originally determined two-and-a-half-mile length to just over one mile (6,800 feet).

In December 1891, Adams and Sellers had narrowed down their prospects and asked for detailed bids from six respected electric companies, including Thomson-Houston, Edison General Electric, and Westinghouse Electric. Based on the initial proposals, which Westinghouse had called "free information," the commission now knew what they wanted: ten 5,000-horsepower turbines to place deep in two central stations, each of which would run an electric generator, resulting in a combined 100,000-horsepower payload. The scale of the project was well beyond anything in existence. Each of the six electric companies Adams and Sellers had solicited bids from began to put together an elaborate plan to be submitted sometime in the next year.

In the meantime, Adams and Rankine purchased two miles of land along the Niagara River, 1,500 acres to be used for dozens of factories, along with a plot of land to develop a small town for workers, called Echota, designed by renowned architect Stanford White.

Tailrace construction marched on for two years until December 20, 1892, when work finally came to an end. The result was the creation of the largest water tunnel in the world, complete with six hundred thousand tons of excavated rock and sixteen million bricks lining the tunnel to fortify its framework. Unfortunately, twenty-eight men had lost their lives in the process.

During the construction of the tailrace, another hydropower project had been taking place in the San Juan Mountains of Telluride, Colorado. The struggling Gold King Mine had decided it needed cheap energy, leading them to contact Westinghouse Electric about a single-phase alternator that could harness power from the 320-foot waterfall in the area. A Tesla single-phase alternator and seven hundred dollars' worth of copper wire spread over three miles of rough terrain helped the Gold King Mine capture three thousand volts of electricity, without a glitch, for the entire year in 1892. George Westinghouse knew this Gold King Mine success would help his position, and he told Adams in the fall of 1892 that he would be submitting a bid. Westinghouse also knew that the success or failure of the World's Fair would be watched closely by Adams and Sellers.

In December 1892, Westinghouse formally offered a fully detailed two-phase AC system to the Cataract Construction

Company. Less than a month later, General Electric came through with its own offer, strikingly similar to the Westinghouse plan, with the only noticeable difference being the fact that GE's proposal involved a three-phase alternating current system.

Thomas Edison's absence as a major shareholder and creative force of General Electric worked against the company's proposal, along with GE's inexperience with a proven and functional large-scale AC system. GE was fighting against great odds.

When Adams and Sellers had the proposals in hand—four total—they began to review each plan and undertake experiments to test the validity of their claims. On January 9, 1893, Sellers and Johns Hopkins professor Henry Rowland ran tests on Westinghouse's alternating current generators and transformers.

Rowland praised the workmanship of the Westinghouse machinery, the company's vast knowledge of alternating current, and the fact that Westinghouse and Nikola Tesla owned all the critical AC patents.

Coleman Sellers, after visiting a General Electric plant to test their three-phase system, concluded, "I should incline to the biphase on account of its greater simplicity and its adaptability to a broader field of usefulness."

After running tests on all the other proposals, Adams began to discreetly correspond with the electrical genius who knew alternating current like no other: Nikola Tesla. In his letters to Adams, Tesla made it clear that his ownership of almost every critical AC patent could not be overlooked or devalued. In no uncertain terms, Tesla explained that Westinghouse's proposal could not be ignored, prompting Sellers to conclude in his twenty-five-page report, "I am not aware of any claim to ownership in this country of what can stop the owners of the Tesla patents from commanding the market. . . . no foreign company can secure the Cataract Construction Co. against all losses from patent litigation."

In early May 1893, with the opening of the Fair dominating George Westinghouse's attention, he learned that his company's blueprints and documents about the prices, labor costs, and details of both the World's Fair and the Niagara plans had been stolen. Westinghouse immediately sought and was granted a warrant, which led to the discovery that a Westinghouse draftsman had sold the plans to General Electric for thousands of dollars. The draftsman was arrested and General Electric was soon found guilty, though GE representatives claimed they had only been trying to see if Westinghouse had infringed on *their* plans.

On May 8, the Pittsburgh district attorney announced conspiracy charges along with his intent to seek a grand jury indictment of General Electric, including the directly named Charles Coffin. A defensive Coffin adamantly denied any involvement in the crime, and in the end he was removed as a defendant, and the Pittsburgh jury found themselves deadlocked.

Then, on May 11—less than two weeks into the World's Fair—Adams and the Cataract Construction Company shocked all four of the electric companies who had submitted plans. In a generic form letter, Adams informed all four companies that their services were no longer needed, as they had appointed their own electric consultant, Professor George Forbes, who was set to design a generator to power their 5,000-horsepower water turbines.

With the World's Fair in full blossom, George Westinghouse did not have time to directly approach Adams and Sellers about this extreme and abrupt about-face. Instead, Westinghouse kept the Fair in focus for most of the summer of 1893, while Forbes spent the same time working on the Cataract dynamo design.

On August 10, 1893, Coleman Sellers, who had been named president of the Niagara Falls Power Company, announced that Professor Forbes had designed a dynamo and transformer that would be used for the plant. In a déjà vu move, Sellers and the Cataract Company once again invited interested electric companies to bid on the contract to manufacture and install its generating machinery.

On August 21, mentioning that he needed to see what Forbes had produced before composing a practical proposal, Westinghouse sent one of his top engineers, Lewis Stillwell, to Niagara to tour and inspect the Forbes designs. It took little time for Stillwell to conclude that Forbes's designs were so helplessly flawed that he could not see any feasible way his company, or *any* company, could construct the machinery. It simply wasn't realistically practical.

As Westinghouse and his team reviewed the Forbes blueprints that Stillwell had brought back to Pittsburgh, Westinghouse immediately relayed the news to the Cataract Company that "mechanically the proposed generators embodied good ideas," opting to apply a thick coat of generous professionalism to his statement, but "electrically it was defective and if built as designed," he flatly explained, they "would not operate." Westinghouse added that the low frequency Forbes had planned would force lights to flicker and flash on and off, and the power was far too low to run a host of other electric devices it would need to run. He summed up his report with the reality that the hyper-elevated 22,000 voltage was far too high, and insulation issues would surface, resulting in an unsolvable problem.

Coleman Sellers and Edward Dean Adams received the Westinghouse report as if a blaring alarm had just sounded, one that was unable to be shut off. It was clear to Adams and Sellers that they needed the expertise and the full breadth of knowledge—not to mention the patents—that only Westinghouse Electric & Manufacturing could offer. If the detailed report wasn't evidence enough that they were making a mistake, the success of Westinghouse's alternating current at the World's Fair served as a clincher.

So it was that three days before the World's Fair closed, on October 27, 1893, George Westinghouse finalized an agreement—complete with a signed contract—to take charge of the Niagara Project. The War of the Currents had been won.

The final blow had been struck, and alternating current and George Westinghouse were the last combatant left standing.

This also meant that Tesla's teenage vision of using Niagara Falls to generate power was about to come true. Nikola Tesla had done it. He'd lost countless dollars by tearing up his royalty contract, but he knew that without doing so he would never have seen his work achieve its full potential. Finally, the Serbian immigrant had realized his American dream.

■　■　■　■

The year 1894 was a busy one for Westinghouse Electric & Manufacturing. There was no more competition in the electric battle; the only fight was the internal battle to perfect the machinery and the alternating current system that'd be utilized at Niagara Falls.

Professor Forbes was "let go" by the Niagara Falls Power Company when Westinghouse made it clear that he and his engineers held no confidence in the man's work. Without Forbes, the Westinghouse team built the first two 5,000-horsepower generators, which were five times more powerful than the generators employed at the Fair. This was completely new territory to travel, but Westinghouse and his crew found their way; they were up to the challenge.

Finally, on August 26, 1895, the first Niagara dynamo came to life at Adams Power Plant in Niagara Falls. Soon after, the second dynamo started up and sent electricity to the first commercial customer, the Pittsburgh Reduction Plant. While there had been difficulties determining the best system to use leading up to August 1893, as well as many obstacles to overcome during 1894 while the team worked to perfect the machinery and its operation, the first month of operation held nothing but success. Everything was proceeding as the electric experts had hoped.

Cataract Construction Company president Edward Dean Adams decided it was time to show off his plant to some esteemed visitors. After all, there was money to be made. Why not impress a who's who of the investment world while things were running so smoothly?

September 30, 1895, might have been the day when the greatest collection of wealth was in one place at the same time. That's the day Adams hosted the all-star cast of characters who made up the Cataract Construction Company Board of Directors. With Edward Dean Adams included, the board featured the likes of John Jacob Astor, New York real estate mogul, investor, and inventor, along with seven more of the most celebrated moneymen in the country. These well-dressed, bowler-hat-wearing, cigar-smoking men visited Adams Power Plant and were the first people to receive a guided tour of the astonishing complex.

Over time, others would be welcomed at the Niagara operation with open arms, witnessing the combined power of the falls and electricity. Inventors, scientists, electrical engineers, celebrities—everyone who visited left impressed, often to the point of waxing poetically about the awesome spectacle. Stories, poems, and songs were written about the special place in between two countries.

Adams Power Plant, a symbol of a Westinghouse victory for AC

But one man refused to visit, despite many invitations. The inventor of alternating current himself: Nikola Tesla. From as early as 1892, Tesla had been invited—often begged—to visit Niagara Falls and the plant he had helped inspire.

Why did he choose to turn down the invitations? He'd never overtly answer this question, but perhaps his refusal to visit the awe-inspiring natural wonder had something to do with holding on to those out-of-reach dreams of his. For Tesla, it's possible he preferred to keep Niagara in his dreams, so as to not let it be corrupted by reality's unflinching indifference to human fantasies.

■ ■ ■ ■

July 19, 1896
Niagara Falls, New York

Tesla had been able to put this off for over five years. The offers had been kind, and the hosts' flexibility and generosity in accommodating any of his desires had been more than anyone could expect. Still, he'd managed to stay away.

Until now.

Nikola Tesla stepped off the Glen Eyre and shook his head at the display before him. His old friend and colleague George Westinghouse was by his side, along with a few other friendly faces, like William Rankine, Edward Dean Adams, Westinghouse attorney and friend Paul Cravath, and thirteen-year-old George Westinghouse III. They were all talking to each other in separate conversations, everyone leaning close to the next person, almost shouting into a welcoming ear.

Nikola had no idea what they were saying to one another. The moaning current and thunderous crashing torrent of water over the sides of the cataract made it impossible to hear anything else. He didn't mind. In fact, as he stepped closer to the falls he was thankful that the roaring water drowned out all other noises. This was just as he'd imagined. He stared, debating whether this was reality or one of his flashes of light. Perhaps it was both?

Something pressed down on his shoulder, forcing Tesla to turn and see William Rankine, who smiled and nodded. Edward Dean Adams turned around and gestured for everyone to follow.

Soon after, the group approached an imposing limestone building that appeared to be *covered* with windows.

"Power House Number 1," said Adams as he stopped at the door.

Nikola Tesla looked at the building, designed by Stanford

White, and paused. Did he really want to see what was inside? Or did he want to keep it as it was in his mind?

Tesla entered the building holding his breath. It took only a few moments for the man to exhale, thankful that he'd decided to come inside. Tesla strolled along the specially designed walkways beside the dynamo and closely inspected what he considered a work of art. This wasn't machinery; it was the *Mona Lisa*. He asked questions of Adams and nodded time and time again, recognizing the masterful construction of the powerful machine. They'd done a fine job.

The group was led down to the ground floor to take a look at the other alternating current machinery before taking a fancy elevator down to the wheel pits, where they heard the water rushing through the penstock pipes, along with the shifting water turbines moving with great force.

After visiting the transformer building across the other side of the canal—traveling over a limestone bridge—William Rankine escorted the group to the Cataract Hotel, which overlooked the American side of the falls.

They treated themselves to an early lunch, with various members of the press dying to talk to the honored guests, Nikola Tesla the recipient of most of the questions.

"It is all and more than I anticipated it would be," said Tesla about the plant. Reflecting on the operation he had witnessed that day, Tesla added that "the plant and the prospect of future development in electrical science, and the more ordinary uses of electricity, are my ideals. They are what I have long anticipated and have labored, in an insignificant way, to contribute toward bringing about."

The reporters asked in disbelief if it was true that this was Tesla's first time at Niagara Falls and the plant. "Yes, I came purposely to see it. But, and it is a curious thing about me, I cannot stay about big machinery a great while."

■ ■ ■ ■

January 12, 1897, 10:25 p.m.
Ellicott Club, Buffalo, New York

It had been a long day for Nikola Tesla. He'd agreed to be the guest of honor at this formal dinner after Edward Dean Adams had first told him that he wanted to celebrate a monumental achievement: the successful effort to use Niagara Falls to power Buffalo, New York, since November 15 of the previous year.

But what Tesla assumed would be a quick stop at Niagara Falls followed by a dinner party where he'd mingle for a bit, say a few words, and then retire actually turned out to be a nonstop morning-to-late-night extravaganza of traveling and sightseeing.

They'd arrived at nine a.m. in Niagara Falls, where they were treated to breakfast at the Prospect House Hotel. From there, they'd visited Power House No. 1 once again, followed by a factory-after-factory visit of businesses powered by Niagara.

After visiting Niagara Falls, they were taken by private train to Buffalo for the celebratory dinner.

After hours of eating and drinking and cigar smoking and talking, Nikola Tesla stood up to address the eager crowd.

Hundreds of the most celebrated names in the country waited with bated, cigar-tainted breath for the electrical genius to share his thoughts.

Tesla pursed his thin lips and took a deep breath through his nose. His dark eyes met the crowd as he modestly opened by admitting that he felt as if he wasn't worthy of the honor they'd bestowed upon him. The crowd relented and shook their heads. Then they turned silent, waiting for more.

Tesla urged everyone to allow their actions to be dictated not just by material motivation—which he admitted was an unavoidable force in the will of men—but "for the sake of success, for the pleasure there is in achieving it and for the good they might do thereby to their fellow men."

The crowd applauded for Tesla's fresh perspective. It was genuine, they knew, and not the contrived, affectatious front the rest put on like a glamorous gown meant to hypnotize the senses from anything else. Those who knew Tesla knew his inventive passion was driven by his desire to better society. This wasn't just an ideal for Tesla; it was his primary motivation. After all, this man had given up a pool of royalty riches.

Nikola Tesla paused. He stared blankly, as if he was seeing a flash of light—something that wasn't really there. Then he looked around at the collection of prominent men with that same blank stare and asked for each and every one of them to be "men whose chief aim and enjoyment is the acquisition and spread of knowledge, men who look far above earthly things, whose banner is Excelsior!"

EPILOGUE: AFTER THE STORM

The Niagara Falls victory marked the end of the War of the Currents. Alternating current and the Westinghouse-Tesla camp reigned supreme. As is the case with all wars, the effects lingered long after the fighting had stopped.

Almost a decade after it had ended, a gruesome incident occurred that mirrored the tactics Edison had employed during the electric war. Topsy the elephant was a veteran performer at Forepaugh's Circus and had developed a reputation as a "bad" or "wild" elephant after killing a spectator in 1902. She was sold to Sea Lion Park, which soon became Luna Park, on Coney Island. At Luna Park, Topsy was involved in a series of public incidents of erratic behavior, leading Luna Park owners Frederick Thompson and Elmer Dundy to plan a public execution, at first attempting to charge people admission to witness the killing.

On January 4, 1903, Topsy was strangled, poisoned, and electrocuted with alternating current, the creature's death ultimately resulting from the electrocution. With Edison Manufacturing cameras capturing the execution on film, later played on Edison Kinetoscopes, over the years some casual observers of the video inaccurately attributed the Topsy killing as a product of the War of the Currents. This, however, is not true, as the incident happened far after the back-and-forth battle had ceased, and Thomas Edison was not known to be in attendance at Luna Park on that day. The horrific Topsy execution, though, does symbolize the lingering effects of the hard-fought war in the years that followed.

Topsy the elephant is electrocuted in public at Luna Park

After the electric war had concluded, Niagara continued to fortify its arsenal of generators, and by the first few years of the twentieth century a fifth of the country's electricity was supplied by Niagara, the natural marvel turned scientific breakthrough.

As each decade handed off the present tense to the next, electricity in a residential sense grew, spreading across the nation at a steady pace. The main reason for this slow growth was the fact that the cost of electricity was too high for the average citizen.

On a commercial scale, electricity fostered massive profits by way of increased productivity. Factories produced more and more goods, which allowed eager consumers to add to their quality of living. Thus, the first few decades of the twentieth century included a gradual increase in the average person's standard of living. Society was prospering, and so were businesses.

Nearly every aspect of business, and society in general, utilized electricity—alternating current electricity. Like water dropping into the Niagara cataract, money poured into the bank accounts of electric companies who sold alternating current. The fight to dominate the electric world was, without much hyperbole, a fight to run the future world. These visionaries—Westinghouse, Tesla, and Edison—had the foresight to understand what would result from winning the war. In turn, their vigor to win made their actions more and more vicious. For this wasn't just a temporary competition; it was a battle that would continue to pay off for whomever came out victorious.

Except for Nikola Tesla, that is.

■ ■ ■ ■

The Serbian wizard of electricity would not rake in that money hand over fist like many of the others involved in the War of the Currents. Tesla couldn't have been surprised by this, since he had ripped up his royalty rights that would have served as an endless supply of income. It was a sacrifice that cost his bank account dearly, leaving him penniless during the final years of his life, but it was also a sacrifice that allowed alternating current to achieve its ultimate potential.

Tesla gives a demonstration of wireless power transmission, Columbia College, New York, New York

Tesla lectured on a regular basis and was a sought-after speaker. He continued to push his creative, inventive ideas, but many people found his post-AC concepts odd. One of Tesla's obsessions materialized in 1901 when he began building the Wardenclyffe Tower in Shoreham, Long Island. This massive structure was 187 feet high, with a large dome made of conductive copper mesh topping the edifice. Underground, the shaft of the tower pushed down into the earth over a hundred feet, with iron piping stabbing down another three hundred feet. Tesla aimed to use Wardenclyffe as a wireless transmission station, intending to send messages across the Atlantic Ocean to England, in order "to telephone, to send the human voice and likeness around the globe." But in true Tesla form, he got caught up in his own mind, and he soon envisioned the transmission of wireless power overseas. According to Tesla himself, the tower was "adequate for the transmission of virtually any amount of energy."

Tesla's grand scheme required more money than he could secure. Construction dragged on and costs piled up. To make matters worse, Tesla's past caught up with him when his old debts with the Waldorf-Astoria came back to haunt him. In arrears to the tune of twenty thousand dollars, Tesla gave two mortgages on Wardenclyffe to George C. Boldt, manager of the Waldorf-Astoria. Unfortunately, Tesla couldn't manage to make any payments, and he soon lost possession of Wardenclyffe to Boldt. Before the strange tower could ever be used, Boldt decided there was more value in the destruction of the tower, so in July 1917 he had Wardenclyffe demolished and the steel sold for scrap.

Wardenclyffe Tower

Tesla found himself obsessed with the concept of the wireless transmission of energy, and specifically, another breakthrough technological device: the radio. As was the pattern for Tesla, the failure to secure a patent or gain public or financial backing while he was experimenting and, most say, inventing the radio, left him off the patent ledger as the inventor of the radio, at least while he was alive.

Instead, Guglielmo Marconi would receive initial credit for the radio. Ultimately, Nikola Tesla's public image would be that of an "also-ran" in his many scientific and inventive battles. Even his victories occurred too late for him to enjoy them, as evidenced when the Supreme Court ruled that Tesla was the *true* inventor of the radio . . . the same year of his death (1943).

Tesla became an American citizen in 1891, a proud moment for the Serbian immigrant. In fact, with all the acclaim and respect he'd earned as an inventor and scientist, Tesla often said he found his citizenship to be his most cherished accomplishment. He valued being an American citizen over any other distinction he'd received.

One honor Tesla did receive in 1916 was, ironically, the Edison Medal, which signified "meritorious achievements in electrical science and art."

Nikola Tesla worked alone for much of his life after the alternating current victory, with paid assistants as his primary human companionship for the active years of his life. George Westinghouse remained a business friend, but no one could ever get close enough to Tesla to be called a true friend, not even Westinghouse.

During the later years of his life, Nikola Tesla finally found his closest and most passionate life partners: pigeons. He'd routinely feed and talk to pigeons, especially outside the New York Public Library. Sometimes he'd sneak ailing or weak pigeons into his hotel room and nurse them back to health. Tesla never married, but—odd as it might seem—one pigeon in particular filled that role. In the twilight of his life, Tesla described this pigeon by saying, "Yes, I loved her as a man loves a woman, and she loved me . . . When that pigeon died, something went out of my life . . . I knew my life's work was finished."

Penniless and a relative mystery to the average American, Nikola Tesla died alone in his thirty-third-floor hotel room at the Hotel New Yorker on January 7, 1943. He was eighty-six years old.

Upon his death, the US government—before his nephew Sava Kosanovic could secure his uncle's belongings—confiscated many of Tesla's scientific documents and his private black notebook, claiming there was an imminent threat due to the fact that the inventor had claimed he'd created a "death beam" prior to his passing. It was not until 1952 that Kosanovic would receive his uncle's papers. Much has been theorized about the papers and what the government did with the knowledge contained in them, but no claim has ever been substantiated. To this day, conspiracy theories abound in relation to the Tesla papers. Just what *did* those secret papers detail? It remains yet another Tesla mystery.

Nikola Tesla, caught up in his studies, sits in front of his Tesla coil transformer.

■ ■ ■ ■

George Westinghouse, like a steady railcar, continued to find success in business and invention, highlighted by the gas shock absorber, which helped make a car ride safe and smooth. Always with an eye on the future, not dwelling on past accomplishments or failures, Westinghouse continued to produce a new patent once every six weeks, culminating in some four hundred patents by the time of his death.

With the stock market crash of 1907, Westinghouse eventually lost control of Westinghouse Electric & Manufacturing Company and the Westinghouse Machine Company. Up to that point, Westinghouse had continued to invest the bulk of his time in his many business ventures. Yet he never lost sight of something far more important to him than business: the people he employed and his family.

Through it all—business successes and failures—Westinghouse and his wife remained happily married and close to each other, along with their son.

Westinghouse's piece work and incentivized stipends led other companies to do the same, and his promise to give Saturdays and Sundays off helped contribute to the traditional work-free weekend for most American companies.

Revered by his employees, those in the business community, and those in the electric fraternity, Westinghouse was awarded the Edison Medal in 1912 for "meritorious achievements in the development of the alternating current system." Awards didn't mean as much to Westinghouse as did the purpose of his work. He summed up what success and professional achievement meant to him when he said, "If some day they say of me that with my work I have contributed something to the welfare and happiness of my fellow man, I shall be satisfied." Indeed, Westinghouse had every right to feel satisfied.

George Westinghouse died on March 12, 1914, and a large segment of the population mourned a great loss.

■ ■ ■ ■

While Westinghouse and Tesla had gained a clear victory in the AC/DC feud, Thomas Edison would be the ultimate winner in the public's retrospective viewfinder, going down in history as the father of invention and the star inventor of the Gilded Age.

Edison greatly prospered in life, even after the direct current defeat, inventing and patenting a seemingly endless list of items still used today (in all, he held 1,093 US patents at the time of his death), which include the motion picture recorder and viewer (the Kinetograph/Kinetoscope) and the alkaline storage battery. He also dabbled in concrete and iron ore, with relative success in both ventures.

An Edison Kinetoscope—used for playback, often in Kinetoscope parlors

Thanks to the Kinetoscope and the phonograph, Edison essentially established a substantial and profitable entertainment industry. He ran his own movie studio—the Black Maria—where he produced a number of silent pictures, leading up to *The Great Train Robbery* (1904), which marked the first time a film followed a narrative structure about a real event. This success led to the birth of the "movie theater" and ultimately the long-lasting impact of Edison's work included the launch of both the entertainment and movie industries.

Over time, Edison has been revered as the pioneer of the industrial surge in the late nineteenth and early twentieth centuries, and rightly so, based on his entire body of work. Long after his death on October 18, 1931, he would be studied in classrooms and cherished in the country he'd helped advance in many ways. Due to the light bulb, the phonograph, the movie camera, and the invention process itself, Thomas Edison became a national hero for his accomplishments.

As such, the viciousness with which he fought against Westinghouse and Tesla was pushed between the lines of the history books, hidden as people learned of the Wizard of Menlo Park as only a genius of invention. Appropriate for the Gilded Age itself, Edison's exterior shine and sparkle hid the interior corruption that came with his victory-at-any-cost mode during the War of the Currents.

THE ELECTRIC WAR
·· A TIMELINE ··

- **OCTOBER 6, 1846**: George Westinghouse Jr. is born in Schoharie, NY.
- **FEBRUARY 11, 1847**: Thomas Alva Edison is born in Milan, OH.
- **JULY 10, 1856**: Nikola Tesla is born in Smiljan, Croatia.
- **1859–1863**: Edison works as a newsboy, selling papers all along the Michigan railway.
- **1862**: Edison creates the *Weekly Herald*, a small publication that features local news and gossip. He sells the paper for three cents a copy, or eight cents for a monthly subscription.
- **1864–1867**: Edison works as a traveling telegrapher.
- **1865**: Westinghouse receives first patent, for the rotary steam engine.
- **JANUARY 1869**: Edison announces in the *Journal of the Telegraph* that he's becoming a full-time inventor.
- **APRIL 13, 1869**: Westinghouse issues first air brake patent. Soon after, the Westinghouse Air Brake Company opens near Pittsburgh.
- **JUNE 1869**: Edison receives first patent, for an automatic vote counter.
- **1870s**: Edison releases several inventions, including a telegraph that prints messages on a strip of paper, an underwater telegraphy system for the British post office, and the Edison Mimeograph.

- **DECEMBER 25, 1871**: Edison, twenty-four years old, marries sixteen-year-old Mary Stilwell.
- **1874**: Edison invents the quadruplex telegraph (can send four messages over a wire simultaneously).
- **1876**: Alexander Graham Bell patents the telephone.
- **MAY 1876**: Edison opens his "invention factory" in Menlo Park, New Jersey.
- **1876**: Edison patents the electric pen along with its complete system, Autographic Printing.
- **1877**: Edison invents the phonograph.
- **1878**: Edison files an early patent on the design of an incandescent light bulb.
- **NOVEMBER 1878**: Edison Electric Light Company is formed.
- **NOVEMBER 4, 1879**: Edison files a patent for the incandescent light bulb with carbon filament.
- **DECEMBER 28, 1879**: Edison holds an exhibition at Menlo Park to show off his incandescent light bulb.
- **FEBRUARY 1880**: Edison submits his first patent application for direct current, termed a "System of Electrical Distribution."
- **DECEMBER 1880**: Edison gets permission from New York City government officials to lay lines underground throughout Lower Manhattan.
- **JANUARY 1881**: Edison relocates from Menlo Park, New Jersey, to Manhattan, as does the Edison Electric Light Company.
- **AUGUST 7, 1881**: George Smith, a dockworker, is killed instantly after placing his hands on a generator at Brush Electric Company in Buffalo, NY.
- **SEPTEMBER 4, 1882**: Edison's bulbs light Lower Manhattan.
- **JUNE 6, 1884**: Tesla, twenty-eight years old, arrives in New York City with four cents in his pocket and his alternating current model, which he is eager to show Thomas Edison.

- **1884**: Nikola Tesla begins working at Edison Electric, but he leaves less than a year later.

- **1885**: Tesla Electric Light and Manufacturing is established in Rahway, New Jersey, with partners Robert Lane and B. A. Vail, who control the company and patents.

- **MARCH 30, 1885**: Tesla works with Edison's former patent agent Lemuel Serrell and patent artist Raphael Netter on his first patent, an improvement to arc lights to eliminate flickering.

- **NOVEMBER 1885**: Westinghouse and Reginald Belfield disassemble and rebuild a Gaulard-Gibbs AC transformer, turning it into the modern-day transformer.

- **JANUARY 8, 1886**: George Westinghouse incorporates the Westinghouse Electric Company.

- **AUGUST 14, 1886**: *Electrical Review* journal features Tesla's Rahway arc lighting project on its front page.

- **1886**: Lane and Vail force Tesla out of Tesla Electric Light and Manufacturing.

- **1886**: Gerry Commission ("Death Commission") is created to investigate the "most humane and approved method" of execution.

- **NOVEMBER 27, 1886**: Adam, Meldrum & Anderson, a department store in Buffalo, NY, opens, using 498 Stanley lights run by Westinghouse's AC system. This kicks off the beginning of the competition between Westinghouse's AC and Edison's DC.

- **1886**: Tesla applies for a patent of the thermomagnetic motor while working various service jobs, including working for Western Union digging ditches for underground cables.

- **1887**: Westinghouse Electric Company partners with Edison competitor Thomson-Houston Electric to install twenty-two Westinghouse transformers.

In addition, Westinghouse Electric Company secures contracts for sixty-eight central stations.

- **APRIL 1887**: Tesla opens Tesla Electric Company with partners Alfred S. Brown and Charles F. Peck. Tesla now works on developing his alternating current system.

- **OCTOBER 1887**: Edison Electric Light releases its annual report detailing the dangers surrounding AC. The eighty-four-page report becomes *A Warning from the Edison Electric Light Company*, which is distributed to reporters and executives of various lighting utilities companies.

- **LATE 1887**: Copper prices nearly double in price from ten cents per pound to seventeen cents per pound, significantly heightening costs for Edison's direct current system.

- **NOVEMBER 1887**: Dentist Alfred P. Southwick writes to Edison, asking him to vouch for the use of electricity as the most humane method of execution. Edison declines.

- **DECEMBER 1887**: Edison writes back to Southwick, now endorsing electricity using alternating current, thereby linking his main competitor, Westinghouse, to the death penalty.

- **MARCH 12, 1888**: The Great White Hurricane slams the East Coast, killing four hundred people and cutting off telephone and telegraph communication due to heavy rain, sleet, wind, and snow.

- **APRIL 15, 1888**: Fifteen-year-old Moses Streiffer is electrocuted by a loose telegraph wire in New York City. The US Illuminating Company is later charged with neglect.

- **APRIL 28, 1888**: Fred Witte dies after touching a United States Company arc lamp.

- **MAY 11, 1888**: Thomas H. Murray, a Brush Electric Company employee, is electrocuted by a severed electric wire while working.

- **MAY 16, 1888**: Tesla presents his AC motor at the American Institute of Electrical Engineering Convention and gains national praise.
- **JUNE 5, 1888**: Harold P. Brown has a letter published in the *New York Evening Post*, demanding alternating current over three hundred volts be outlawed, along with other proposed restrictions. The letter is read before the New York City Board of Electric Control.
- **JUNE 7, 1888**: Westinghouse writes to Edison, inviting him to come to Pittsburgh to form a truce. Edison declines five days later.
- **JULY 1888**: Tesla and Westinghouse agree to work together on alternating current.
- **JULY 16, 1888**: Westinghouse presents a letter to the New York City Board of Electric Control, explaining that 127 AC central stations had been created in two years' time without incident, while several of Edison's DC stations reported fires in that timeframe.
- **JULY 30, 1888**: Harold P. Brown meets with over seventy people from the press and representatives of various electric companies at Columbia College. Here, Brown electrocutes first animal (a dog) using AC.
- **SEPTEMBER 1888**: New York state legislature designates electrocution as its new mode of capital punishment.
- **NOVEMBER 15, 1888**: Dr. Frederick Peterson informs Medico-Legal Society of New York that both AC and DC can kill, but he prefers AC.
- **DECEMBER 6, 1888**: The *New York Times* declares alternating current the "most deadly force known to science."
- **JULY 1890**: Edison testifies that the electric chair is more humane than hanging.
- **AUGUST 6, 1890**: William Kemmler is put to death at Auburn Prison for murdering his wife, becoming the first person to be executed.
- **OCTOBER 1890**: Baltimore, Maryland, purchases 6,000-light alternating current

system, soon followed by an order for 1,500 lights in southern New York and in Nebraska.

- **OCTOBER 4, 1890**: Initial work begins to harness Niagara's energy.
- **LATE 1890**: World financial markets take a dive, forcing Edison General Electric, Thomson-Houston, and Westinghouse Electric to consider possible mergers.
- **JULY 30, 1891**: Tesla becomes an American citizen.
- **1891**: George Westinghouse convinces Tesla to terminate Tesla's AC patent contract and waive his present and future royalties. Westinghouse agrees to continue sharing Tesla's polyphase system with the world.
- **1892**: Edison Electric board members urge Edison to consider switching to alternating current, but Edison objects.
- **FEBRUARY 5, 1892**: Alfred O. Tate, Edison's personal secretary, informs Edison that Edison General Electric has merged with Thomson-Houston. The company is renamed General Electric, leaving Thomas Edison with no controlling interest.
- **MAY 16, 1892**: General Electric and Westinghouse Electric both bid to light and power the 1893 World's Columbian Exposition in Chicago. Westinghouse Electric wins the bid.
- **DECEMBER 1892**: Westinghouse offers a fully detailed, two-phase AC system to the Cataract Construction Company. A few weeks later, General Electric makes a similar offer, but with a three-phase AC system.
- **JANUARY 1893**: After Westinghouse loses appeals to use Edison-style bulbs for the 1983 World's Columbian Exposition, his patent on a Sawyer-Man "stopper" bulb is ruled unique and noninfringing, allowing him to move forward on lighting.
- **JANUARY 9, 1893**: Tests are performed on Westinghouse's AC generators and transformers for the purpose of the Cataract Construction Company. All tests are met with praise.

- **1893**: The World's Columbian Exposition is held in Chicago, Illinois, completely powered by Tesla and Westinghouse's alternating current. The Electricity Building demonstrates the AC system.

- **MAY 1893**: Westinghouse learns documents containing details of both the World's Columbian Exposition and the Niagara plans have been stolen. It's learned a Westinghouse draftsman sold the plans to General Electric for thousands of dollars. GE representatives claim they were only trying to see if Westinghouse had infringed on *their* plans.

- **MAY 11, 1893**: The Cataract Construction Company announces they have appointed their own electric consultant, Professor George Forbes, to design a generator to power their 5,000-horsepower water turbines.

- **1893**: Tesla's writings, edited by T. C. Martin, titled *The Inventions, Researches and Writings of Nikola Tesla*, are published.

- **AUGUST 10, 1893**: President of the Niagara Falls Power Company, Coleman Sellers, announces that Professor Forbes has designed a suitable dynamo and transformer. The Cataract Construction Company once again invites bids for the contract to manufacture and install its generating machinery.

- **AUGUST 25, 1893**: Tesla passes 250,000 volts of alternating current through his body at the World's Columbian Exposition as a demonstration to prove its safety.

- **OCTOBER 27, 1893**: Westinghouse finalizes an agreement to take charge of the Niagara Project, using Niagara Falls to generate an unheard-of amount of power. Nikola Tesla is a major part of this project.

- **AUGUST 26, 1895**: The first Niagara dynamo comes to life, sending electricity to the first commercial customer, the Pittsburgh Reduction Plant.

- **JULY 19, 1896**: Tesla tours Niagara Falls with Westinghouse and four others.

- **JANUARY 12, 1897**: Tesla is the guest of honor at a formal dinner to honor the successful effort of powering Buffalo, New York.

- **AUGUST 31, 1897**: Edison patents the kinetographic camera, a device for viewing moving pictures without sound.
- **1901**: Tesla builds Wardenclyffe, a 187-foot tower, in Shoreham, New York.
- **JANUARY 4, 1903**: Topsy the elephant is strangled, poisoned, and electrocuted with alternating current.
- **1907**: Stock market crashes and Westinghouse soon loses control of Westinghouse Electric & Manufacturing Company and the Westinghouse Machine Company.
- **1912**: George Westinghouse is awarded the Edison Medal for "meritorious achievements in the development of the alternating current system."
- **MARCH 12, 1914**: George Westinghouse dies in New York City at the age of sixty-seven.
- **1916**: Tesla awarded the Edison Medal for "meritorious achievements in electrical science and art."
- **1917**: The Wardenclyffe Tower is destroyed.
- **OCTOBER 18, 1931**: Edison dies at the age of eighty-four in West Orange, NJ. At the time of his death, there are 1,093 patents in Thomas Edison's name.
- **JANUARY 7, 1943**: Tesla dies at age eighty-six, alone in his hotel room. The US government confiscates many of Tesla's scientific documents and his private black notebook.
- **1943**: Supreme Court rules Tesla is the *true* inventor of the radio. Guglielmo Marconi had initially received credit. Many people still debate who the actual inventor is.
- **1952**: Sava Kosanovic, Tesla's nephew, obtains his uncle's papers, almost a decade after Tesla's death.

·· ACKNOWLEDGMENTS ··

Even a brilliant person like Nikola Tesla needed others to help him bring his ideas and inventions to reality. Such is the case with a writer. An author might have the knowledge and skill to tell a story, but to actually create a book, a wide assortment of people are needed. This said, I have a number of people to acknowledge who helped me craft this book.

I'd like to thank Brianne Johnson for urging me to write narrative nonfiction, which was not on my radar until she mentioned it. Bri considered my writing style, knowledge base, and platform, and then posed the idea to me. I've run with it ever since and haven't looked back. Thank you, Bri.

Thanks as always to my best writing buddy Tracy Edward Wymer for always being there, as a critique partner and as a friend.

A big thank-you to Miss Jenny Burke at the Community Library of Dewitt and Jamesville for rounding up a ton of books for my research. Sure, it took me a few hand trucks and forklifts to transport all the books, but without them this book wouldn't exist.

My editor, Christy Ottaviano, and her whole team deserve a great deal of thanks for seeing the potential in a couple of books about the Gilded Age. It took a detailed proposal and a sizable chunk of this book to get Christy to sign me on, and for that I am forever grateful. Christy, I hope you are proud of the work we have done, and the final product on these pages. Here's to all our future projects together as well! A specific thank-you to Jessica Anderson for all she has done along the way, and to my amazing copy editor, Bethany Reis, for the massive effort she put into this book. Bethany, what you did was nothing short of magic. You are a very talented editor.

Finally, my family is my lifeline, made up of my wife, Shelby; my children, A.J. and Savannah; my mother, Gerrie; my step-father, Garry; my brothers, Jeff and Tim; and my collection of nieces and nephews. All of you have been there for me as I put this book together, so thanks for all you've done to help me. Thanks, also, to my mother-in-law, Lydia, and all the Staffords for their love and support. Finally, my father told me long ago, during a difficult conversation, that maybe one day I'd write a book. He certainly was right about that.

·· BIBLIOGRAPHY ··

"Adam, Meldrum & Anderson, a Brilliant Illumination." *Buffalo Commercial Advertiser*, November 27, 1886.

Adams, Edward Dean. *Niagara Power: History of Niagara Falls Power Company, 1886–1918*. Niagara Falls, NY: Printed for the Niagara Falls Power Company, 1927.

Baldwin, Neil. *Edison: Inventing the Century*. New York: Hyperion, 1995.

Barrett, John Patrick. *Electricity at the Columbian Exposition*. Chicago: R. R. Donnelley, 1894.

Brandon, Craig. *The Electric Chair: An Unnatural American History*. Jefferson, NC: McFarland, 1999.

Brown, Harold P. "Electric Currents." *New York Times*, December 18, 1888: 5.

Burgan, Michael. *Nikola Tesla: Physicist, Inventor, Electrical Engineer*. Minneapolis, MN: Compass Point, 2009.

Carlson, W. Bernard. *Tesla: Inventor of the Electrical Age*. Princeton, NJ: Princeton University Press, 2013.

Conot, Robert E. *A Streak of Luck*. New York: Seaview, 1979.

"Copper." *Electrical Engineer*, 18 (February 1888): 42.

Daly, Michael. *Topsy: The Startling Story of the Crooked-tailed Elephant, P. T. Barnum, and the American Wizard, Thomas Edison*. New York: Atlantic Monthly Press, 2013.

DeGraaf, Leonard. *Edison and the Rise of Innovation.* New York: Sterling Signature, 2013.

Delano, Marfé Ferguson. *Inventing the Future: A Photobiography of Thomas Alva Edison.* Washington, DC: National Geographic Society, 2002.

"Died for Science's Sake." *New York Times,* July 31, 1888: 8.

Dommermuth-Costa, Carol. *Nikola Tesla: A Spark of Genius.* Minneapolis, MN: Lerner Publications, 1994.

Dyer, Frank Lewis, and Thomas Commerford Martin. *Edison: His Life and Inventions.* New York: Harper, 1910.

Edison, Thomas A. "The Dangers of Electric Lighting." *North American Review,* 149 (November 1889): 625–33.

"Edison Says It Will Kill." *New York Daily Tribune,* July 24, 1889.

"Edison's Electric Light." *New York Herald,* March 27, 1879. Thomas Edison Papers, Rutgers University.

"Edison's Newest Marvel." *New York Sun,* September 16, 1878.

"Electric Death." *Buffalo Evening News,* April 4, 1889: 1.

Essig, Mark. *Edison & the Electric Chair: A Story of Light and Death.* New York: Walker, 2003.

Forbes, George. "The Utilization of Niagara." *Electrical Engineer,* 18 (January 1893): 65.

Freeberg, Ernest. *The Age of Edison: Electric Light and the Invention of Modern America.* New York: Penguin, 2013.

Garrison, Webb B. *Behind the Headlines: American History's Schemes, Scandals, and Escapades.* Harrisburg, PA: Stackpole, 1983.

Gernsback, H. "Tesla's Egg of Columbus." *Electrical Experimenter,* March 1919.

"In a Blizzard's Grasp." *New York Times,* March 13, 1888: 1.

"Inhuman!" *Buffalo Evening News,* August 7, 1890: 1.

Israel, Paul. *Edison: A Life of Invention*. New York: John Wiley, 1998.

Jay, Mike, and Michael Neve, eds. *1900: A Fin-de-siècle Reader*. London: Penguin, 1999.

"Jealousy." *Buffalo Evening News*, April 2, 1889: 1.

Jehl, Francis. *Menlo Park Reminiscences* Vol. II. Dearborn, MI: Edison Institute, 1937.

Jonnes, Jill. *Empires of Light: Edison, Tesla, Westinghouse, and the Race to Electrify the World*. New York: Random House, 2003.

Josephson, Matthew. *Edison: A Biography*. New York: McGraw-Hill, 1959.

Lanier, Charles D. "Two Giants of the Electric Age." *Review of Reviews* (1893): 41.

Leupp, Francis E. *George Westinghouse: His Life and Achievements*. Boston: Little, Brown, 1918.

Levine, I. E. *Inventive Wizard: George Westinghouse*. New York: Julian Messner, 1962.

"Like a City Mourning." *New York Times*, October 16, 1889: 1.

Lomas, Robert. *The Man Who Invented the Twentieth Century: Nikola Tesla, Forgotten Genius of Electricity*. London: Headline, 1999.

"Magnificent Power Celebration Banquet at the Ellicott Club." *Buffalo Morning Express*, January 13, 1897: 1.

Martin, Thomas Commerford, and Nikola Tesla. *The Inventions, Researches, and Writings of Nikola Tesla*. New York: Electrical Engineer, 1893.

McCabe, James D. *New York by Sunlight and Gaslight: A Work Descriptive of the Great American Metropolis*. Philadelphia: Douglass Brothers, 1882.

"Met Death in the Wires." *New York Times*, October 12, 1889: 1.

Moran, Richard. *Executioner's Current: Thomas Edison, George Westinghouse, and the Invention of the Electric Chair*. New York: Alfred A. Knopf, 2002.

"Mr. Brown's Rejoinder, Electrical Dog Killing." *Electrical Engineer*, 7 (August 1888): 369.

"Mr. Edison Is Satisfied." *New York Times*, February 21, 1892: 2.

"Niagara Is Finally Harnessed." *New York Times*, August 27, 1895: 9.

O'Neill, John J. *Prodigal Genius: The Life of Nikola Tesla*. New York: Ives Washburn, 1944.

"Power of Electricity." *New York Times*, July 16, 1889: 8.

Prout, Henry G. *A Life of George Westinghouse*. New York: American Society of Mechanical Engineers, 1921.

Satterlee, Herbert Livingston. *J. Pierpont Morgan: An Intimate Portrait*. New York: Macmillan, 1939.

Seifer, Marc J. *Wizard: The Life and Times of Nikola Tesla: Biography of a Genius*. New York: Citadel, 1996.

Stead, F. Herbert. "An Englishman's Impressions at the Fair." *Review of Reviews*, 8 (July 1893): 30–31.

Stillwell, Lewis B. "Alternating Current versus Direct Current." *Electrical Engineering*, 53 (May 1934): 710.

Stross, Randall E. *The Wizard of Menlo Park: How Thomas Alva Edison Invented the Modern World*. New York: Crown, 2007.

Tate, Alfred O. *Edison's Open Door: The Life Story of Thomas A. Edison, a Great Individualist*. New York: Dutton, 1938.

Tesla, Nikola. *Experiments with Alternate Currents of High Potential and High Frequency: A Lecture Delivered before the Institution of Electrical Engineers, London*. New York: McGraw, 1904.

———. *My Inventions: The Autobiography of Nikola Tesla*. Eastford, CT: Martino Fine, 2011.

————. *Very Truly Yours, Nikola Tesla*. Radford, VA: Wilder, 2007.

Tesla, Nikola, and John T. Ratzlaff, ed. *Tesla Said*. Millbrae, CA: Tesla Book Company, 1984.

"The Alleged Theft of Westinghouse Blueprints." *Electrical Engineer*, 14 (June 1893): 587.

"The Westinghouse World's Fair Exhibit." *Electrical Engineer*, 25 (January 1893): 100.

Westinghouse, George. "No Special Danger." *New York Times*, December 13, 1888: 5.

Wetzler, Joseph. "Electric Lamps." *Harper's Weekly*, July 11, 1891: 524.

"A Wireman's Recklessness." *New York Times*, May 12, 1888: 8.

"World's Fair Doings." *Daily Interocean*, May 17, 1892: 5.

INDEX